HEALING FROM NARCISSISM:

A JOURNEY THROUGH THE STAGES OF RECOVERING YOUR PERSONALITY FROM NARCISSISTIC DISORDER, DISCOVER COMPASSION AND LOVE FOR OTHERS. GET OVER THE ADDICTION OF SELF-OBSESSION

Author: Dr. Rachel Bancroft Psyd

Introduction

Narcissism is a tough nut to crack. It's not easy to say why narcissists act the way they do, and there is no singular reason. Within these pages, you will be given a peek inside the extreme your inner world, allowing you to better understand your thought processes and motivations.

If you have ever worried that you yourself might be a narcissist, these chapters will help you to self-reflect on that question and decide whether or not treatment through clinical therapy is a wise course of action to take.

If you had a narcissistic parent, the psychological effects can be so severe that it can haunt you for the rest of your life and even cause you to adopt the same qualities and thereby pass them on to *your* children, causing an endless cycle.

This book is intended to shed some light both on the underlying disorder as well as the resources and options available to those who are in this situation. It will hopefully prove as an incredibly valuable resource to anybody who finds themselves in this tragic situation.

Above all, don't be afraid and neither be discouraged. You will find not only information but encouragement and power in this book. You will be well equipped to get a much better understanding as to diagnosing and treatment of the disease. Life isn't over just because you have Narcissistic Personality Disorder. There are new powerful ways to treat it that you deserve to know about so you, or your loved one, can live a happy, healthy and safe life.

The biggest obstacle is making the change yourself, and finding a way to better who you are by being better to the people around you.

This book will help you figure out the answers to dealing with your condition, regardless of whether you bully, manipulate, control, or criticise. The information given in this book will help you fully understand what the narcissistic disorder is, the various types of narcissism, different ways to deal with your condition in the various aspects of your life, and how you can regain your sense of control.

Once you are armed with the right information, it won't be difficult to deal with your personality. When you start to follow a couple of simple practices, you will see that interacting with others doesn't have to destroy them. Once you understand the various tips and tricks given in this book, you can regain the control you thought was lost.

It is time to take corrective action and empower yourself to regain your control once again. Finally, you'll get plenty of guidance on how to stop narcissistic abuse in its tracks and move towards personal healing. So, if you are ready to take the leap, let's get started.

Chapter 1: Pathological Jealousy, Lies and Insecurity

Pathological Jealousy, Anger and Envy

Jealousy is a major emotion experienced by those with narcissism. They want to be the best, and they view themselves as superior. If a person comes along that is truly better at something, jealousy kicks in. For example, a group of men are playing basketball. It is natural to want to be the best, but for most people, they learn to accept when another player is better. However, for the narcissist, this isn't possible. This can result in intense jealousy to the person who outplays.

Any time their delusions of grandeur are questioned, or another person is shown better at something, narcissists can experience humiliation. This can cause them to become angry and lash out at the people they feel humiliated them.

Anger is one of the most common emotions that a narcissist experiences. This anger can also become rage if the person is not able to control it. Someone may become angry for the smallest things, such as a friend taking two minutes to talk to someone else when they are around. Anything that takes the attention from a narcissist is enough to trigger anger. Feeling inferior, criticism and jealousy or anger can also trigger anger in a narcissist.

The narcissist feels that everything they have is the best and that they absolutely deserve the best of everything. If they see someone with a newer or nicer car, for example, this can trigger them to become envious. In some cases, this envy can become almost obsessive. They will focus on it, think of it constantly and try a number of ways to essentially one up the person who has something that they are envious of.

Emptiness is another emotion that is common with narcissism. It can make them feel unsettled and uneasy. Remember that the narcissist needs to feel as though they are powerful and the centre of attention. When these are not happening, the emptiness can creep in. This can cause them to do something to bring the attention back to them, such as belittling the person who is currently getting attention.

Happiness is not an emotion they really experience. Instead, they tend to view feelings of power as happiness and not the genuine happiness that someone who is not a narcissist feels. For example, when a person gets a new job that they wanted, they feel happy that they are getting this new opportunity. However, for a narcissist, the happiness is more of a feeling of power and feeling that getting that job will elevate their status.

INSECURITY

The insecurities from which Narcissistic Personality Disorder are based creates jealousy and envy in such people. It can also be true that they think others are just as envious of them as they are of other people. There is anger at anyone who has proof of actually being better or more successful and so they are angry that they too do not have this same proof and glaring evidence of their own heightened level amongst others. Envy is a core feeling and thus it is one of the rawest feelings a narcissist can have.

For them, nothing is worse than realising they are not as great as they think or say and that there are others that are. This conflicts with the idea of their superiority and they have a hard time processing it. Envy does not merge well with the façade they have created. In order to preserve their ideas without revealing their insecurities, they turn their envy into resentment. This leads to higher levels of accosting toward the party they are envious of. The threats, criticisms, and harsh words could be the beginning of a very dark cycle.

Narcissism is certainly not a good thing, but it can be much darker than it appears in textbooks. When thinking of the danger involved, it is generally not physical, and because of this, those around the narcissist might not realise the danger they are in. If harm is caused, it is usually emotional, and it can take longer for this to takes its toll or appear evident.

A narcissist does not care about the feelings or well-being of the people around them. When they lash out, their goal is not to cause emotional harm or pain. It is simply to preserve the image of themselves that they are trying to portray.

Initially, the emotional harm caused by a narcissist might not feel significant. However, over time, the impact can start to build until it begins to diminish the victim's self-esteem and overall joy. This is especially true if the narcissist is the person's close friend, relative or significant other since their treatment and opinion is viewed as important.

The vulnerable narcissist makes a major show of being hurt and treated badly and they seem to care a little that their partner recognises how the world treats them badly and stands against the unfairness with them.

If you are a narcissist, you see the world through a mirror where everyone you meet admires you, flatters you, is envious of you and obeys you without question. When you look in a different mirror, you still see yourself as the person to be admired, flattered, envied and obeyed. You have no other filter that distinguishes your real image from your imagined image.

Therefore, if other people do not see what you see, if they fail to admire, to flatter, to envy and to obey, you feel like they are threatening you. When someone assaults you, you have no choice but to fight back and fight back you will.

You will fight back fiercer and harder and better than your attacker. You will rage and roar and you will win their submission.

In the narcissist's mirror, they are always larger than life. They are always bigger than anyone around them, they are always smarter, they are always more successful. They need to know that and be constantly reassured of it to stay stable in their world. When you contradict a narcissist, it moves well past a simple disagreement.

As a narcissist, you must stop your attacker cold at the first assault, because should you allow them to land even one more blow, they could shatter you and you might never recover.

Did you know that narcissistic people are prone to road accidents? According to a study by Bushman and colleagues, the researchers have found that almost all road fatalities are because of narcissism, which leads us to believe that being narcissistic, especially the 21st century, can lead to death. People with NPD are highly impulsive. They have no regard for rules of safety because they have a strong sense of gloriousness within themselves. Narcissistic people see themselves as gods and goddesses. Some of them might think, but they will not get hurt from aggressive driving because they can avoid death. But this is only a fruit of their distorted reality. They believe that they are untouchable, and they are not easily silenced. So, they prove their point and being aggressive on the road by cutting lines, aggressive overtaking, and many more.

The biggest difference between the world of the narcissist and the non-narcissist is how other people are viewed.

If you are a narcissist, other people are basically inconsequential in your life. They are there to serve you and admire you. If they do anything other than that, they are annoying. Everyone around you is less intelligent than you are, and less accomplished. Not one of them could hold a candle to you, even on your worst day.

Other people are to be used to get you to where you want to go. They have no real value to you other than in the context of usefulness. When they cease to be useful, or when they impede you in any way, they must be eliminated from your inner circle.

These other people, who see value in everyone, have a lot of trouble understanding that you see value in no-one. In times of conflict, they will innocently appeal to your better nature, totally uncomprehending that what they see is your nature and it has only one other side, and that is the rage side and it is worse.

That is why it is so difficult to be true and lasting friends with you. In a normal friendship, people support each other. They see the finer things in each other, and they understand that there is an implied informal contract of loyalty, of "being there" for each other.

As a narcissist, you find such a concept laughable. They should be glad to serve you, and if they need you, that is not convenient. You will not be there.

If, as a narcissist, you have a disagreement with someone, they will often be shocked at the depth of your anger and disdain and try to appeal to your better nature. They will beg you to consider someone else who will be hurt by the decision, they will assume that despite your anger, somewhere within you is what they would call a "heart," a nature where goodness simmers and rises to the top on occasion.

As a narcissist you can be incredible cruel. You can turn against your long-suffering spouse, your own children, your parents, your neighbours and your friends and not lose a minute's sleep over it. While those on the other end of your rage mourn and cry and consider ways to reach you, you have no such thoughts. People who hurt you have no right to expect anything at all from you, let alone compassion or change.

As a narcissist, when people talk to you, you hear only the part of the conversation that relates to you. If they discuss other things, you drown them out with your thoughts about yourself.

If as a narcissist you fight with someone because they are ignoring or annoying you, and then you return to your normal life, you are always surprised if that same person comes back at you with a sneak attack. You do not expect that. Once you are done with them, you expect that they will be done with you.

Narcissists lack what other people describe as a conscience, that niggling inner voice that warns you your behaviour is wrong or what you are contemplating is bad. As a narcissist, you have no inner voice. You have only a developed pattern of thought that tells you if you steal or kill, you will be punished in the courts of law for it. And that is the only thing that keeps your behaviour and your disdain and contempt for others in check at all.

As a narcissist you tell so many stories about yourself that many of them are contradictions, sometimes even within the same conversation.

If you are a narcissist, you cannot understand the world of the non-narcissist where they willingly and openly praise others and appreciate their talents without being threatened by them. Non-narcissists will support an up-and-coming musician because they believe they have much to offer; they will purchase art from a student because they believe it to be good and they want to encourage the young person to continue on the path they have chosen.

As a narcissist, however, you compare yourself to everyone who comes in contact with you and you must always feel that you are better than they are.

As a narcissist, you are not happy to attend such pastimes as concerts or art show openings because they are either a waste of your valuable time, or if you see something that you think just might be better than what you can do, you will fall into a deep depression.

The narcissist has a dark and negative view of life. They are constantly concerned that their needs and their superior position is unchallenged, they are agitated and stressed. They believe the world is a nasty place and that the people they meet are out to get them.

As a narcissist, you have an opposite view of the world. You are always primed for attack, always looking after your own survival. You want to be superior, successful, and powerful and you fantasise about that endlessly. Calmness and serenity are for the dead. You know the world is a rotten place and that you cannot trust the people in it.

You are extraordinarily competitive in a way that your non-narcissistic co-workers and friends cannot comprehend.

If you are a narcissist, it is not easy for you to share. You believe you are entitled to take what is around you and you cannot understand the purpose that could be served to share it with others. Your tendency to exploit your world stretches to the people in it. You will shamelessly use them and discard them as they are useful to you.

Chapter 2: Diagnostic Testing and Treatment for NPD

How to identify whether or not you are a narcissist

Let's now take a look at the symptoms marking that disorder and determine whether or not your narcissism has augmented to being a personality disorder.

YOU CAN'T STOP TALKING ABOUT YOURSELF.

A narcissist loves to talk about their own accomplishments, and show off proof of what they have achieved. They might direct attention to their trophies, during a social gathering at their place, for example, or interrupt someone mid-sentence to share about an award they won at work that day. They want you to admire them, so they will try to gain this admiration any way they possibly can. In some cases, if you don't comply with this desire, they may resent or attack you. Other narcissists may simply respond in a passive-aggressive way.

NO RELIABILITY AND IMMEDIATE GRATIFICATION

Narcissism is not just a mixture of rudeness and an overblown sense of self. Since this is a type of personality, it can be anything from a quirk in someone, to a serious medical problem, involving unexpected or counterintuitive actions. Not every narcissist out there is dislikable or obnoxious. Actually, a lot of them are appealing and charming, while others simply have deep wounds that they are trying to hide. The issue here is that typically, it's hard to stand even speaking with them.

THEY BREAK RULES AND VIOLATE BOUNDARIES.

A narcissistic person might enjoy the thrill of violating social niceties, rules, or even laws. They are seemingly unable to accept that they should respect the order put in place.

They might cut people in line at the store, refuse to tip the waitress, or simply shove someone out of the way while walking down the street. They don't typically stop to think about how these actions could hurt others, and instead do it because it's what they want. They see strangers as anonymous people that just don't matter, and often view those close to them in a similar way. Until someone can do something for them, they feel no need to be polite or respectful.

A narcissist does not always have the most professional of ethics, even at work. This could take the form of acting inappropriately with a client at work (by asking for their phone number, or insulting them in a passive aggressive manner), or taking things from the office because they can. Going on to brag about these actions later is another sign.

THEY USE PEOPLE FOR THEIR OWN GAIN.

Exploitation, or using others for their own gain, is another symptom of Narcissistic Personality Disorder. Narcissists find that other people are easier to take advantage of because such people either conform to their idea of being more superior or others bend to their will strictly because of how everyone else sees and treats them highly. Having a sense of being better and smarter than everyone, it is easy for someone with this disorder to use people for their own benefit. In their eyes, these people are not worthy to be respected and as such, it seems reasonable to use them to their benefit. Again we have a symptom that connects to other symptoms quite simply. Exploitation comes from their belief that they are owed what they are demanding and they will constantly demand more.

THEY HAVE A HABIT OF PUTTING OTHERS DOWN.

For a narcissist to come across as superior, and hide their fears of inadequacy and insecurities, they often engage in putting down other people. In their minds, this makes them come across as acceptable and desirable in the eyes of others, by comparison.

People who are targeted by a narcissist might be described as "clueless" managers, "inferior" people, or "flawed" friends or exes. The way they describe others is nearly always from a place of perceived superiority. Many different people have had narcissistic bosses.

AVOIDANCE OF COMMITMENT.

It can be confusing when you're romantically interested in someone who appears charming and affectionate toward you, but doesn't want to take the relationship any further after some time has passed. The good news is, if you are involved with someone who displays traits of narcissistic personality disorder, there are skills and strategies you can use to restore respect, balance, and health to yourself.

SELF-IMPORTANT

They will see themselves as having a higher level of importance and will exaggerate this importance. Bragging, exaggerating their worth, and focusing a great deal on the aspects they think are significant, can make this symptom very apparent. The person will often belittle others because they see no reason not to. In their eyes, they are already more important and superior and so they see no problem in pointing it out or expecting this to be common knowledge. Nothing in particular has to occur or be present for the person to see themselves this way. They already have the thought cemented in their mind and little can be done to dissuade them. When in a group, they will often push to be the centre of attention, or walk away with the expectation that they will be followed. They will assume that people will do as they are told or will instantly respect them for what they say and do.

DELUSION

With Narcissistic Personality Disorder, they often live in a dream or false reality. This is kind of an overall issue as it puts all the other symptoms together in a synthetic world. Most of their beliefs are falsified in their own mind. This, in turn, allows a screen to cover everything around them in order to colour the world in such a way that they find themselves having a significance that normally would not exist. The delusion is then set to allow for someone to see this imagined reality as an allowance for their arrogance. Often this can play out in such a way that the person will have people that do abide by their assumed superiority, giving credence to the false reality, and thus making the symptoms and the disorder more difficult to dispute. The false reality also acts as a protective barrier for a narcissist who is this way due to childhood trauma or abuse. Creating a world in which they are above what they have experienced, are better because of what they have gone through, or a reality completely separate from the one they actually had is their way of coping. If a person has suffered in such a way that they have decided upon a world in which better things happened to them and they came out on top, it can seem difficult to change this state of mind. In truth, it can also be rather dangerous.

FINICKY STANDARDS

Narcissists believe that they can only be understood by and able to communicate with people they think are as exceptional as they are. This drastically lessens the number of people they think are even worth talking to. Being that they use inflated sense of self to confirm their personal ideas of who they are, they will not have any issue with people who do the same. On top of that is the idea that if someone is as exceptional as they are, they strive to surpass this person in order to prove their own self-worth.

HIGH EXPECTATIONS

Narcissistic Personality Disorder will leave the person demanding more from others. They will come to expect the admiration and honour they believe they deserve. Offence is easily taken at anyone who does not bow to them and their believed superiority. If they are able to scam or take advantage of someone, they will continue to do so because they feel that if they did it once, then they must do it every time in order to keep up the appearance they originally set forth. The idea of demanding more is a way to confirm their authority or higher position over the people around them. They do not see a problem in expecting more and, in fact, may see a person as better for adhering to their growing needs and expectations. Though the people that endure this constant and ever-growing demand may see themselves as less for bending to the will of someone they may even consider as underserving of their help, the narcissist will rarely notice any growing resentment.

DEMANDING SPECIAL TREATMENT

Favouritism and immediate compliance is an automatic expectation from people around someone with Narcissistic Personality Disorder. They expect their treatment to be above that of anyone else and see no reason for this to ever be different. They assume they can get away with more and often do simply because people are either afraid of them, annoyed by them, or just want them to be happy and get rid of them. With the compliance of those dealing with the narcissist, the special treatment becomes an expectation. This leads to them constantly expecting more each time. Giving in to someone's preference, though, does not always mean they are doing it out of kindness or bowing down to people with this level of arrogance and sense of self.

LACK OF EMPATHY

Empathy is something that narcissists usually lack. Their inability to understand and feel what others feel makes them incapable of relating to others. This further goes back to the idea that they are better than everyone else. They do not see people around them as being smart enough to have the level of thinking and emotions that they do, so they ignore the importance of those emotions and feelings.

This leads to the arrogance, or haughtiness, that comes with narcissism. The smug looks, pretentious tones, smirks of disdain, and so on, show their disbelief of anyone else's importance while accentuating their own. Arrogance is the basis of most of the narcissist's actions. Arrogance is also a result of the reactions of the people they exploit, see as below or less than them, and the purposeful interactions with people of a higher standing. The cycle is brutal in this way. Arrogance and self-importance creates the false reality in which they believe they are better than everyone else, which leads to how they treat and see others, which then leads into a greater arrogance.

Treatment for Narcissistic Personality Disorder

Although there are treatments for people with NPD, this can be a very difficult disorder to eradicate. Most therapists find that helping the patient manage the symptoms is the best course of treatment for people with NPD. There are several reasons this disorder can be difficult to deal with in a therapeutic setting.

First, these traits are so ingrained into the person's psyche, it is quite hard to change them. This is primarily because behaviour started forming at a very young age, when most personality traits develop in childhood.

Second, the nature of NPD can make it extremely difficult to treat. People who suffer from this disorder believe themselves to be smarter than others around them, more capable, and deserving of special treatment. This means that they don't usually recognise that there is a problem at all. Usually, only a concerted effort by the people in their lives to point out their issues will bring someone to therapy. Of course, for therapy to be successful, the patient must admit that there is a problem. Also, once they are in therapy, the patients tend to devalue the therapist, making it difficult to form the therapeutic bond between patient and therapist that can help the patient relate to the therapist, which allows them to explore their disorder.

Many psychiatrists and psychologists have difficulty treating someone with NPD because they often have a blatant disregard for their doctors or therapists, believing that they know more about what is wrong than the therapists. They may even try to intimidate their caregivers to prevent them from helping the patient change.

There are different approaches to psychotherapy that can help people with Narcissistic Personality Disorder.

BEHAVIORAL THERAPY

This method is simply defined as changing what a person does you to help of a therapist. Behavioural theorists have proposed aversion therapy in which a behaviour is paired with some form of punishment. The common use of this therapy is to help people quit substance abuse disorders. Behavioural Therapists also use the process of desensitisation, also known as the process of a gradual introduction of the stressful stimulus. This is usually done to people who are experiencing trauma and phobia. As for the case of people with Narcissistic Personality Disorder, a distress-causing stimulus for them is imperfection, loneliness, lack of attention, and criticisms. To slowly change the perception of people towards these aspects, a gradual introduction could be used.

COGNITIVE THERAPY

This form of therapy has been developed to help clients to change their self-defeating thought patterns and behaviour. For many years, the process of cognitive behavioural therapy has been pro to help people with various forms of psychological disorders.

Another technique for successful cognitive therapy is known as Graded Exposure Assignments. In this method, the therapist will allow the client to be systematic and the approach their greatest fears. It allows the patients to deal with their own fear and control their emotions during a very threatening situation. Your system at the exposure, the client starts to master these feared situations one-by-one, until he finally can control his emotions and thoughts as the event arises.

Activity scheduling is also a common way to help people increase the onset of behaviors that they should be doing more. In several cases of people with Narcissistic Personality Disorder, they should be interacting with people more.

Another important technique introduced by cognitive therapy is mindfulness. It is a technique they borrowed from Buddhism in which a person is taught to disengage from ruminating or obsessing about negative things. Mindfulness is also a way on how people can be aware of their reality. So, they can match their goals to their actual capabilities in place of success.

SUPPORT GROUPS

Support groups can be either a good thing or a bad thing with Narcissistic Personality Disorder. On one hand, like with group therapy, they have the chance to meet others with the same condition. This allows for the understanding of how it is to be on the opposite side of a narcissist, and to understand how anyone can be afflicted by this. The downside is that most support groups are online. With the virtual barrier protecting you even more from facing truths or facts, the delusion can often be fed from these experiences more than thwarted. The key is to have as group moderator/s people that have learned to accept that they are not above everyone else, that they are plagued by insecurities, and that others feel the same way they used to. These can act as guides. They can tell people what they used to think about themselves and others and then what helped change their opinions and perspective.

HUMANISTIC THERAPY

This form of therapy focuses on the person's nature rather than comparing his experiences of behaviour to the similar problems of others. Humanistic therapy perceives the person as a whole, and it structures its foundation from the client's perspective himself, who is an active observant of his own actions. Humanistic therapy is commonly used to treat people with personality disorders, depression, anxiety, addiction, and schizophrenia. Through this process, a person can reach his full potential by acknowledging his strengths rather than his weakness, by searching for his purpose, and by setting motivational goals.

INDIVIDUAL THERAPY

This is generally not a short-term prospective, and someone with NPD could spend years in therapy to achieve all these goals. However, that is no reason to get discouraged. Some changes can take place very quickly if the patient is interested in change and is willing to do some work. The changes can result from the patient being willing to monitor their behaviour and modify it when it is unacceptable.

As with most conditions warranting psychotherapy, the first step is an actual one-on-one session with a therapist. This gives the therapist a chance to evaluate the needs of the patient and the patient has the chance to have the exact issues identified by a professional. With a one-on-one therapeutic session, the patient does not feel the need to maintain any perceived reputation. There is also the guarantee of confidence from the therapist, giving the patient the ability to trust the therapist not to belittle them. The idea of sitting down and talking about problems with someone though, is not always something a sufferer of Narcissistic Personality Disorder is going to be very open to. In their mind, there is no problem except for the people they think are threatening them or what they stand for. A therapist will be able to ask them what exactly it is they feel about other people, how they interact differently with other people, and what feelings they think other people are dealing with. Opening up the possibility of understanding others can help someone with Narcissistic Personality Disorder be able to have some empathy towards others and ultimately be less self-centred.

GROUP THERAPY

Working with a therapist in a group setting is also a great idea for someone with narcissistic personality disorder. This gives the person the opportunity to interact with others, in a controlled setting, to teach them how to interact effectively. When a person suffering from NPD engages in group therapy, they can learn self-control when dealing with others, have other patients like them point out when they are being unreasonable, and act out confrontations with a therapist trained in dealing with this disorder. By doing so, the patient can learn better functioning with others. It also enables the patient to learn to identify others as separate from themselves, under the guidance of other patients who are further along in the process and a trained therapist. This can help to accelerate the learning process for the person with NPD. Also, patients further along in the therapeutic process can help newer patients. Individuals can learn a great deal from each other, when given the opportunity. Group therapy is a good way for people with Narcissistic Personality Disorder to see their own symptoms and actions through someone else, someone they may not have even considered to be at their level.

Being that someone with this disorder would have a strict criteria of people they believe are as smart, as attractive, as successful, or with whatever similar attributes, as they are, group therapy can be a chance for them to experience their own inadequacies through others with the same condition.

MEDICATION

Although there are many psychiatric medications available on the market, most do not directly treat the symptoms of NPD. Instead, medications can be prescribed to deal with indirect issues that a person with NPD may have, such as anxiety (especially when going through therapy for low-self-esteem issues) and depression. Many psychiatrists feel that psychotropic medications are not helpful in any way to someone suffering from NPD.

HOSPITALIZATION

In extreme cases, someone with severe NPD may be hospitalised in a psychiatric facility. This could happen when a person's symptoms are so severe that they become a danger to themselves or others. Because of the volatility of people with NPD, it is possible that they could place themselves in danger because they have difficulty telling what a real danger is and may take behaviours to the extreme. Their lack of impulse control could contribute to dangerous behaviours. Also, if someone upsets them, it is possible that they could take their aggressions out against someone else. Again, their inability to control their impulses may lead them to physically lash out at others. It's recommended that any hospitalisation for NPD be short term and should be concentrated on dealing with the specific symptom that brought them to the hospital in the first place. Long-term hospitalisation has not been shown to be effective for people with NPD.

How to Handle NPD in Therapy?

There are instances when clients are referred to a psychologist without their consent or their idea. Knowing that people with Narcissistic Personality Disorder see themselves as perfect, they will believe one that they do not need any psychological intervention. Heck, they do not acknowledge that they are mentally sick. During which cases, we need to learn the tricks to handle patients like this so they can help us help them grow and heal from their abnormality. But how do we do it to patients with Narcissistic Personality Disorder during treatment?

According to some experts in the field, to handle a narcissist person successfully before treatment, kiss up to that person and gain a bit of his trust. Do this in the form of praise, affirmation, and approval. Compliments sound good to them, especially when they observe that they have your full attention. As a psychologist, use this to your advantage. Keep on leaning towards them without saying anything about the purpose as to why they are brought to therapy. Narcissists love to talk about themselves. So, lure them into opening up about their childhood experiences or their difficulties as a child. Sooner or later, you will probably hit something sensitive, and they start to overdramatise. Then, employ the element of comfort. Tell them about the importance of their healing to get over these negative thoughts and experiences. Make them understand the importance of doing therapy for their own good. You can tell them that undergoing therapy will give them the capability to achieve their dreams to make them feel better. Narcissists love to hear when they feel like they are taking advantage of the efforts of other people. But as you move on to the process of therapy, they will soon have values realisations about themselves and their reality. They might not show this at first because they have pride, but you will observe a gradual improvement of their attitude towards your approach in therapy.

If the practitioner is in a position to advice, use the "What would people think?" approach. We all know that narcissists are preoccupied by the way people judge them. Ask them what people would think when they found out that the client has this kind of weakness. Encourage them to receive help from you. But first, make them believe that you are not that kind of person who would use their information to ruin them. Narcissistic people can be very paranoid, so gain their trust. Approach them in a way that they would perceive you to be non-threatening to their ego. Pretend that you worship them, and you love what they do if you have to. But it should only be in the hopes to get them to open up their inner thoughts to you. Show them a non-disclosure contract if need be and explain to them your duties and ethical code of conduct as a practitioner. Moving forward to the "What would people think" bait, make them believe that these weaknesses and insecurities may be used against them by other people. This is why they need to be fixed as soon as possible. This is where you start to introduce therapeutic methods to change their lifestyle and their cognitive processes. Soon enough, they will begin to show changes in behaviour and personality.

Whatever you do in dealing with your clients, always be patient and determined. Keep an open mind and realise that all of that need help. You might be the only key for them to survive in this cruel world. I know how much it stresses you out when dealing with cases like these, especially Narcissistic Personality Disorder, which is considered as cancer in society. They can cause a terrible headache as they don't know how to acknowledge their disease. But remember that they are victims too. If the rules were reversed, wouldn't you want to be helped by other people when you have a serious medical condition? It is our job as a practitioner to provide competent service to different people. And to do this, we should commit to our societal obligations and do whatever we can to provide the service that our clients need.

However, there are times when a practitioner needs to terminate the client-therapy relationship. You need to endorse the patient to another practitioner when your methods and treatments are not working anymore. To help the patients fulfil their highest potential, they need a practitioner who can provide what is best for them. If you know it within yourself that you cannot help the person in need, do not deny them the service. Instead, explain to them that they need to see another professional to experience a more active recovery from the psychological illness. The downside is, this could be very difficult to take on the part of your client. So, you need to give the closure they need to start over with a new therapist.

How to Approach Choosing the Right Therapy

The right therapy for someone with Narcissistic Personality Disorder will depend on their situation and who is affected the most by their issues. If there are relationship issues, then a couples' therapist would be more appropriate. If the disorder is causing issues in social situations, then a group therapy session might be more useful. Despite the course taken, a one-on-one session would be pertinent as the first step in any therapeutic sense. The therapist that the patient sees initially will be able to guide them to the next step in the process. They can evaluate the situation, the problems being faced, and what the disorder hinders in the patient's life. With their objective and professional opinion, the therapist can have a more neutral standing on any issue that plague their patient's life. Sometimes guidance is necessary to get through situations that one cannot fully understand.

For a narcissist, the biggest problem still, is admitting that there is a problem in the first place. With the idea that they have a superior position in life, they may not want to have their perspective changed. A person suffering from Narcissistic Personality Disorder is not going to want to go see someone that will bring out their insecurities and point out the ways that they are not better than everyone else. This topples the whole foundation of the disorder. Once the step to even see a therapist is overcome, then a bigger focus needs to be made on the aspects of life affected by the problems that they are dealing with.

Chapter 3: Accepting the truth

Understanding Narcissism

Narcissism is a character trait in which someone displays a heightened over-confidence due to their admiration of themselves; they can simply do no wrong. This is an exaggerated behaviour that breathes and exudes arrogance, pretentiousness, and a deep-rooted ideology of false superiority. "I am special. Everyone else in the world is below me because they are not me". A person who exhibits narcissistic characteristics is often described as being cocky, self-centred, self-absorbed, and rude. They view life as a playground for manipulating emotion, as an untapped market in which to exploit and to bend truth at will. They can be viewed as "winners", but they are crude people to be involved with due to their self-described perfection. So, too, are they liars. Their success – in most cases – is because of their total and complete disregard for other people and their feelings. Or rather, narcissists will push past people no matter what those people are feeling. They view other people as obstacles. We are, basically, their next hurdle to get over. They would most likely push us off the edge of a top-floor balcony if it meant that they would get just a little more ahead of everyone else.

Narcissists are the perennial interrupters of conversation. They constantly crave the limelight; they feel as if they deserve everyone's attention at each and every single turn. They want to be seen. They want to be heard. They want to be the leading figure in any small gathering, work circles, friendship circles, and among the large crowds. They are the people who ooze confidence in every moment. They are very charming people and more often than not, they are quite funny, very sarcastic. They are good company in public, but once at home and in their own respective comfort zones they shed their charming skins for the emotionally depraved, ostentatious colors that they don when returned to their private and intimate places. They use manipulation and excessive, yet believable, lies as a tool to such an extent that narcissists are almost fanatical individuals in regard to their use of such methods.

Narcissists have such a deep self-belief burning within them. But beneath all of that lies a person who has been deeply affected by life. Narcissists are people, though pretty hardcore ones, who have been shaped by past trauma, past experiences, or past abuse, which, in turn, has crafted them into a person with such anxiety that the line between nervousness and abandonment has morphed and blurred into a singularly, individualistic focus that the adulation that they are constantly seeking is due to their inner mental conflicts that were borne from a lonely and possibly unloved childhood. This has made them develop what we could call external spotlighted arrogance. The definition of this is, simply, a spotlight. Some form of inner spotlight that externalises itself – or switches on - when it feels like it needs to be seen. It burns so bright that it forces people to shift and focus all undivided attention on the narcissist. This trait or behavioural characteristic, if looked at from a psychological perspective, is most common in children below the age of 10. It is that need to stand out from the rest, to get attention, whether that is from your parents, your family, your friends; it's a phase our brains go through during early childhood development that can be best linked to the behaviour-type of being boastful or to brag about something. In a narcissist's case, what they are essentially bragging about is themselves.

We all know a narcissist. They could be our mother or our father; they could have been this way for as long as we can remember and have left us, now in adulthood, shattered, confused, exhausted. They could be our brother or our sister; they were always showered with praise, always told that they were the star – they were serial winners and developed an egotism that has become the prospective difficulties in our lives, still affecting us at this very moment. They could be a work colleague or an employee. But what are the roots of narcissism?

Narcissists tend to view themselves quite differently when compared to others, and they often make those around them feel inadequate and devalued. Here's the kicker—a narcissist always wants everything to be about themselves. You might not mind showering a one-year-old infant with all your attention, but you will start to mind when a 35-year-old demands the same level of attention and achieves it at your expense.

Narcissists easily victimise others by just being who they are, and it is unlikely they will ever change. This might seem rather severe, but until you deal with a narcissist, you will not realise how toxic such individuals can be. To understand NPD, you must first understand the way narcissists think about themselves.

Where does narcissism come from

Narcissism usually develops in early childhood. I have heard people say many times that narcissistic behaviour reminds them of a toddler throwing a tantrum. I tend to agree with this statement based on personal experience. It seems, the emotional trauma responsible for narcissism occurs around the age of a toddler, hence the narcissist's ability to handle emotions gets stuck at that level of mental development. That explains their dangerous emotional immaturity, doesn't it?

We all get exposed to trauma during the early stages of our development. It's simply inevitable. Trauma can result from something as simple as not being picked up by our parent as a baby or being fed against our will. It could also result from something more severe like our mother leaving us at the kindergarten for the first time, which can cause a long-lasting fear of separation. Our parents fighting and screaming at each other in our presence can leave its imprints on our subconscious mind, too. So, what kind of trauma produces a narcissist?

Growing up with an either overbearing and/or completely neglectful parent can warp a child's mind and cause them to be narcissistic adults later in life. A parent can be overbearing when it comes a child's performance in school and neglectful when it comes to the child's emotional needs.

The trauma of a narcissist is the perceived lack of control. The inability to acknowledge their own emotions makes a narcissist extremely uncomfortable. Admitting one "wrong" thing about themselves would make them feel as though everything is wrong. So, every abusive and manipulative action they take only serves one purpose: to feel in control. The root of their toxic behaviour towards you has nothing to with you, it has everything to do with them. If you play close attention to their accusations, you will see that they in fact, project their behaviour, fears and doubts on you. A narcissist may often lie, yet accuse you of lying all the time, no matter how much proof you present that they are wrong. They may feel as if everyone is out to get them and that they always get the short end of the stick, so they project their subconscious beliefs on you by accusing you of plotting schemes against them every time there is a simple misunderstanding.

You must keep in mind that narcissists never truly learned how to express and process their emotions. Their parents may have been overly protective and proud of them – but only when they fulfilled their parents' expectations. One could try to do some research about the past of the narcissist in question. Though it usually is difficult to get a clear picture. It's very difficult to find the truth about a narcissist, especially when their parents admit to not having been able to handle their child.

In many cases one or both of their parents may display some narcissistic traits, too. That does not mean, however, that the children of a narcissist are bound to become narcissistic as well.

At the end of the day, it's not up to you to determine why the person that treated you so badly has become who they are today and it also not necessary for your recovery process. However, what is necessary for your recovery process is that you are aware that it's definitely not your fault in any way that they are a narcissist, and with that you are not responsible for their chronic toxicity.

This can be an environmental cause that can lead to a forced image of perfection later in life. Another aspect is early childhood abuse. One way to deal with abuse is to see yourself as above it, too clean for it. Taking an abusive history into account, narcissism acts as a wall to prevent being hurt further in the future. Despite the several ways the disorder can be environmental, there is also some belief that the trait can in fact be hereditary. With genetics, though, seeing a specific behaviour trait can be difficult. Often, though it may seem genetic, it is more over the way that parent or grandparent was raised that gives them the condition. This brings up the question of actual genetics. Science has yet to come to a clear conclusion on that though. Studies have not been able to come to a solid conclusion, and with many different conditions, it is hard to see which is environmental and which is genetic.

Majority of the cases of Narcissistic Personality Disorder, though, always points back to the parents who raised the child. Whether it is neglect, abuse, overprotection, rewarding for insignificance, Munchausen, or even the parent giving the child a hypochondriac disorder or a sense that they are superior, the child's behaviour is usually created at an early age. With such a deep-seated basis and such a long time for growth, this makes the disorder even harder to overcome later in life. Changing someone's perspective of how they should see the world when they were raised and to see it differently can be a nearly impossible task. This also can cause more behavioural and personality issues. Taking away the one or only, defence someone has constructed in order to deal with trauma can then lead to an exposed and vulnerable feeling that can cause depression and/or anxiety. What happens then is the person goes from being narcissistic to high risk Avoidant Personality Disorder, agoraphobia, social anxiety, self-harm and even suicidal, or an intention of hurting others. People using narcissism to cover an abusive or traumatic childhood would have to be approached with the utmost care.

Even if the issues are genetic, there is really no direct way to treat genetics over a learned behaviour cycle. Hereditary behaviour issues are something a species line has evolved to. Somehow that series of genetics has evolved to see itself as more significant than others. Whether this has to do with the biological mating habits or some kind of protective reaction of the line, it is part of who the person is. Just as someone is likely to have a stronger inclination to be a leader or one who helps people for a living, being someone who sees themselves as above others will already be in their head from early childhood. As with a learned behaviour, this comes from one or both parents. If the parent(s) has the same genetic disposition, then they will raise the child with that frame of mind, once again, the person is locked in a cycle. Being both genetically superior and raised to believe that they are so will be the prime persona of the person and thus something which is not easy to change.

Can Narcissism Be Cured?

Since narcissism is classified as a personality disorder, those in the psychological community have created tools and methods to allow the narcissist to better cope with their abnormal emotions and behaviours. However, no magic pill can simply stop someone from being a narcissist.

It can also be hard to treat a narcissist because it is not easy for them to admit they are wrong and need help. They can view someone recommending they get help as a betrayal. A psychologist or psychiatrist can also be perceived as a threat to their distorted fantasy life and sense of superiority.

Should a narcissist agree to seek treatment, psychotherapy is generally where it starts. This involves different forms of talk therapy, including individual and group. This works to aid the person in working toward healthier relationships because they can learn to better relate to others. Over time and with regular therapy, they may be able to find relationships more enjoyable, intimate and rewarding. This therapy can also help them understand the root of their emotions and what is driving them to distrust others, compete or despise others.

Keeping up with treatment is also important. This means that any medications should be taken exactly as directed and all therapy sessions should be attended. This all contributes to the narcissist being able to remain focused on their goal. A professional may set up series of small goals that they will help the person to work toward. As they accomplish each of the mini goals, it can help them to see that progress is being made, so should a setback occur, they can see that they are still doing better than they were before.

If the person has any other mental health conditions, or a problem with substance abuse, treatment for these should be tackled. A healthcare professional can help them to determine which additional treatments might be needed and beneficial.

Chapter 4: Return to Humanity

Get professional assistance if you are Damaged-Overcoming Emotional Trauma

Supportive friends and family will always allow you to express how you feel and offer you some form of comfort or advice. When we are surrounded by supportive individuals, we gain perspective and learn to accept and overcome our negative emotions. Choosing who we are going to be close to really makes or breaks us as people. Previously, we have established that narcissists disapprove of their victims' negative emotions. They belittle or dismiss expressions of anger, guilt or sadness. We know that in our relationship with the narcissist, we simply have to be what they want us to be. After all, our real emotions don't exist to them. What happens if you choose to express your feelings in front of the narcissist? You will learn to see yourself through the narcissists' eyes and you will begin to respond to your own emotions in the same distorted way as the narcissist.

Many victims believe at some point in their recovery process that they have become narcissistic themselves. If you are wondering about it yourself, I can assure you that you have not been turned into a narcissist. The fact that you think about such a possibility proves that you are not narcissistic in the slightest bit. A "real" narcissist would never even consider having a personality disorder in the first place. They simply are unable to practice honest self-reflection like a healthy individual. When it comes to mental issues, narcissists are quick to conclude and proclaim that it's everyone else that's having these problems but them. This is so, because the possibility of having mental issues would make them less than what they want to be perceived as. They want to see themselves in a positive way and a personality disorder would ruin the show.

The problem is that the narcissist's distorted perspective doesn't help us to overcome our emotions and grow as a person. The only thing we learn from the narcissist is to judge ourselves for feeling something. Positive emotions are no exception. To a narcissist, emotional people are weak and naïve. They dislike happy people. A narcissist believes that happy people know no hardships – much like a child. Though they may envy cheerful individuals, narcissists will always try to place themselves above such people by pointing out how much more "life experience" they have instead. It's as if a lost sense of joy is what makes a person mature and experienced in life. Anything less than that cannot be taken seriously by the narcissist.

It's quite a sad and dark place to come from but we must learn to respect the narcissist's point of view without getting emotionally involved.

Allow yourself to Grief

Narcissist carry a lot of grief within due to all the pain they weren't allowed to express and their real personality they weren't allowed to show. It hurts deeply to have your character dictated to you despite your attempts to fight off all the wrong claims directed at you. You feel unseen and unheard - or constantly misunderstood at the very least. While it is true that we cannot control how other people see us, it is unfair to be silenced in the middle of an attempt to explain yourself and demonstrate your true character.

Oddly enough, the thought that our true character does not exist in the narcissist's world bears a feeling of relief. Knowing this is incredibly powerful, as it allows us to understand that we don't have to justify our actions or prove ourselves to them - or anyone else who is unwilling to listen to what we have to say, really. Separating our true character from the character others project upon us opens up yet another opportunity to nourish our self-esteem. That being said, no matter how much we want to move on and be fine again, a great deal of healing lies within our ability to turn inward and become present with our emotions. We absolutely must allow ourselves to grieve if we are serious about moving on. This process can take hours, days, weeks or months. It may come on and off, but it is imperative to give ourselves the permission to grieve, no matter how much time it'll take to heal.

It is a very personal, transformative experience. We won't be quite the same once we overcome the deep-seated feeling of grief. It links closely to anger and it is completely normal to get very upset in the process. Whatever emotions come to surface, let them out. It helps tremendously if you have a good friend to talk to, someone who understands and does not judge you. If you do not wish to talk, you may turn to writing, painting, even hot baths help! All you need is time and a comfortable space where you can forget about the world and focus your attention on yourself. There is no right or wrong way to grieve. Treating yourself as you would treat a good friend is the way to go. It's a great thing to finally give yourself the attention you've been denying yourself for so long.

The only criterion for successful healing is honesty. You must be absolutely honest with yourself regarding your thoughts and emotions. Revisit past events in your mind, express how you've felt at those moments and how you feel about them now. As objectively as you can, try to analyse the narcissist's behaviour and explain why they did what they did and why they said what they said based on what you've learned about the personality disorder. Get angry, just try not to act upon it. Define what makes you angry, not why you are angry. The latter will give you more reasons to stay angry, the former, however, gives you an opening to snap out of it and gain an objective perspective instead.

You can also focus on how anger feels in your body – though preferably not while you are in this emotional state. Each emotion comes with physical sensations and recognising these sensations can help get these emotions under control before they get out of hand. Additionally, the objective identification of the physical manifestations of an emotion helps us accept how we feel. Allow yourself to be overcome by an emotion without letting it completely take over your words and actions and avoid criticising or justifying how you feel and think. That's what being present with your emotions is all about. When we are present with ourselves, we don't try to change how we feel, we accept it without judgment.

There's a saying that what we resist, persists. It definitely fits the bill here. The more we try to fight and judge our emotions, the less control we have over them in the end. These same emotions tend to get resolved almost on their own if we take a moment to be with them though. It helps to remind ourselves that each and every emotion is valid, simply because it exists. There can be a lot or nothing to learn from these emotions. And there is absolutely no reason to panic as soon as we realise that we are getting emotional over something either. Don't allow the internalised voice of the narcissist to govern your emotional conduct. It's okay to be you.

Freeing Yourself from Negative Emotions

Anger, jealousy, envy and other negative emotions can permeate your life and cause significant problems. It is important to recognise their existence and then work to be free of them. Freeing yourself from such emotions is a process, and it takes time. Even after you free yourself, you will need to commit to long-term work and maintenance.

Negative emotions are powerful and can quickly become habits if you do not get them under control. For example, if you commonly respond to criticism with anger, over time, this repetition will cause you to become angry any time you are criticised. This can start to impact your relationships, your career and other elements of your life.

Recovery from Shame and Guilt

One of the biggest hurdles to overcome during the recovery process are feelings of shame, worthlessness and fear. Any kind of relationship with a narcissist will leave us in a depressed state where we feel worthless, unlovable and ashamed of ourselves. This is because the narcissist will usually project their own deep-seated feelings of shame onto their victim, creating the same negativity within them. While it may seem that a narcissist does their best to manipulate and break their victim in order to stay ahead of the game, most of the time they simply can't help it. Even though some narcissists truly plot negative schemes in order to create drama, there is no use to get stuck at the stage of merely uncovering the narcissist's negative patterns either, because there is no end to them. Taking note of their more often than not awful behaviour while telling ourselves that they are doing everything on purpose only leads to more feelings of anger and frustration. We are better than that and eventually we all can move on from here.

So, what awful things are we talking about? You are correct, if you guessed "conditioned self-blaming!" Narcissists continuously condition their victim to take the blame for everything they've done or didn't do. It's extremely difficult to catch up on because the conditioning is often done in an otherwise positive situation. A narcissist simply cannot accept that sometimes, it's impossible to predict or understand a person's actions or judgment. Doing so would require them to acknowledge the lack of control over people and their surroundings. And with lack of control being their trauma, they simply can't accept such a reality. I hope you are able to see now why they tend to change and adjust their story in hindsight in an attempt to justify their reactions every single time.

Deeply rooted feelings of shame and self-loathing will likely pull you towards self-sabotage once you begin to rebuild your life. It is not uncommon for victims of narcissistic abuse to feel not good enough when it comes to taking care of themselves. This is a form of learned helplessness, that's been cultivated in our mind by the narcissist from the very start of our relationship with them.

Constant self-doubts and negative self-talk will make it hard for you to stick to your decision to create a better life for yourself. Criticising yourself for not being who and where you want to be in life will make you feel ashamed of yourself and your surroundings. You may also become afraid of success as a result of doubting yourself. While you may want to become successful and take the first steps to achieve your goals, deep down you still believe that someone like you doesn't deserve to be successful.

Comparing your broken self to your ideal self makes positive change seem impossible. To overcome these deep-seated feelings of shame, therefore, you must accept the fact that closing the gap between who you are and who you want to be is a slow process you can learn to fall in love with. You must constantly remind yourself to slow down and take baby steps towards success and self-improvement. It's not a question of lightning-fast results, but rather that of patience and consistency. Overcoming shame means to understand that self-confidence and a positive self-image have nothing to do with other people's approval of who you are and what you are all about. Your achievements in life have little to nothing to do with your personality and value as an individual. How you treat others - and more importantly - how you treat yourself, makes all the difference. Now all of this is just my opinion, but what do you believe?

Self esteem workout

Everyone's self-esteem swings like a pendulum between good days and bad, but normally the radius of the swing is well within normal limits.

For people with perennially low self-esteem however, the radius of the swing in the bad direction goes further and further until it threatens to swing into oblivion and they feel they will drown in despair.

Some signs that your self-esteem is getting dangerously low is when all you recognise in yourself are your limitations and weaknesses and faults. You cannot credit yourself with solving anything, with figuring out life or the challenges it throws at you. You place no value on what you think and wait to hear what others think before you can decide what to do about anything. Everyone around you, in your eyes, is smarter and more accomplished than you are.

In your eyes you are a failure and likely always will be. Success is for other people to enjoy, not you. Even when someone praises you for work well done or how nice you look, you don't believe them. You can't accept nice things being said about you.

Your conviction that you will fail at whatever you try keeps you from trying things that you could actually do. It is a sorry cycle and unfair to you and the person you could be if your self-esteem could swing back and forth in a healthier radius.

On the other end is the growing high self-esteem. Every day your pendulum of emotion swings a little farther to the belief that you are great and successful and better than those around you. Gradually and over a period of time, your high self-esteem swings higher and higher and higher, right off the scale and one morning you wake up to feel so highly about yourself that you have become a narcissist.

At a more reasonable level, of course, a high self-esteem is generally good for you. It means you have more self-knowledge, that you recognise that you have some talents and skills and the ability to use them. Your view of yourself is more accurate than the person who feels everything they touch will be a failure.

When you have a healthy self-esteem, it is not that you believe you are perfect; it is just that you recognise your flaws but believe you have more good qualities than bad ones. You have a balanced personality.

In a balanced personality, you have the confidence to meet life's challenges face to face. You believe you have the capability to deal with life and work and raising a family and all the dimensions that create a full life. You may have moments of doubt, but overall, you function effectively in a busy world.

You have, in essence, a touch of narcissism, but yours is a healthy sense of self that will spur you to take a few risks, achieve some substantial successes, and relate well with people and build genuine, lasting relationships that will support you through your life.

How do you know when your healthy self-esteem is swinging past the radius into unhealthy or overly narcissistic?

When you begin exaggerating your importance and boasting about your accomplishments, you are moving into the danger zone. If that is coupled by your feeling that you are superior to everyone around you, then you are becoming a narcissist.

Gradually you start to feel contempt for those around you. You imagine that you are the only one who really understands what is going on and how to do things properly. You believe you are more gifted and skilled than everyone else.

What you are experiencing is not just a healthy self-confidence but an unnatural love for yourself that covers your hidden insecurities.

The struggle between low and high self-esteem is part of human nature and none of us are immune to it.

To have a healthy self-esteem means you are able to live a full and purposeful life, to develop lasting relationships and to look upon the world as a good place to be. You are open and curious about things, and constantly learning.

You are not afraid to express what you think or what you need. You make decisions easily and you are comfortable with them. You don't have to consult everyone else and beg them to make your decisions for you.

You are not inclined to be consumed with guilt or shame because as a general rule, you behave in a civilised fashion and treat people decently. You are able to forgive yourself if you make a mistake and just as importantly, you have the capacity to forgive others.

Children who have low self-esteem are more likely to feel sad, guilty, angry and ashamed of themselves. They do not believe they really deserve good things if they come their way.

Their behaviour is more negative and they do not perform as well at school. Convinced they are not smart and cannot do as well as their smarter colleagues, they will indulge in self-defeating behaviour. They work themselves up to a high state of anxiety prior to a test, for example, and are unable to perform to their best, even though they may actually have the correct answers. Their boding sense of failure thus becomes a fact.

When they do fail, it is almost as if they are telling themselves, "I told you so." It confirms their negative thoughts about themselves and sends them spiralling still further down the tunnel that ends in negativity and self-fulfilling failure predictions for the future.

Parents have an important job to help their children nurture an inner sense of self-worth and a healthy dose of narcissism to help them have a happier, more fulfilling life.

No matter what they do or what others do, a child must know inside that they are a person of value. We must teach them to be confident in their own worth and not gauge from a comparison to somebody else. In fact, children need to understand that they are valuable in this world and it has nothing to do with how they relate to other people. We must explain to them that no matter how gifted they are, or how beautiful, or how accomplished, there is always someone else who surpasses them in some area.

Knowing what's triggering the feelings about your self-worth is a good first step to addressing them. Now try to analyse what happens to you when you are in the company of those people that upset your value of yourself and if there is something you can do to protect yourself. Are you interpreting the situation correctly? Are your reactions to what is happening rational or irrational?

Once you figure out if your reaction is based on what is really happening, or if your emotions and perceptions, played on by another, are leading you to false conclusions, you will be better able to confront the situation directly.

Other than false perceptions, there are number of other ways of thinking that can threaten your sense of self-worth and cause you to feel bad about yourself without any logical cause. Quite often they are situations you find yourself in because of a certain way of thinking, and that thinking can easily be changed.

When building up your self-esteem always remember that just because you think a thought or have a feeling, that does not make it real. At its extreme, you may say you feel like a failure, but that does not mean you are one. You may feel that the boss is singling you out for particularly harsh treatment, but perhaps the boss is being tough on everyone.

When people don't do the things you expect, do not immediately assume that it is because they don't value you and thus, you are not worthy of value. Things happen in other people's lives that don't mean anything to you, but are extremely upsetting to theirs. A parent who is up all night with a sick child and really needs to be home early today to get them to a doctor may refuse your offer for coffee. You are devastated. Clearly they place no value on your friendship. You are leaping to the wrong conclusion. The person is all wrapped up in their own crisis of the moment and will call you another day when things calm down.

To boost your self-esteem, nothing is more important than staying positive and reminding yourself of all the parts of your life that are good. Keeping a gratitude journal where you take a few minutes each day to make notes of all the things you have to be thankful for is an excellent way to remind yourself of what is working well in your life.

Another self-esteem saviour can be stepping away from yourself, including your innermost negative thoughts, and looking at them from a different perspective. You might write about them rapidly as they cross your mind and record everything in your journal. Some therapists suggest that if you are right handed, you try to write out disturbing thoughts with your left hand, and vice versa, giving your brain a specific cue that you need a different perspective on this thought.

It can also be therapeutic to turn your nagging thoughts into a poem or into a song. Sometimes the very act of creating something around a bad experience can be quite cathartic.

In this case, you can be aware that certain thoughts are troubling you, but your mind also signals that you have had a good meal, the sun is shining on you, the warm breeze cools your skin and there are fragrant flowers in the meadow across the road. Give yourself into what is fine about this moment and instead of doing battle to remove certain thoughts, you instead incorporate the beautiful moments into the present.

A Narcissist's Low Self-Esteem & Why We Stay

Many would assume that a narcissist has a high level of self-esteem, which is why they might be most interested in controlling others, right? It's normal to assume that a narcissistic person wouldn't have any issues with confidence, since this is what they work so hard to portray. Yet the mask crumbles behind closed doors. This is the main reason why it is so "crazy-making" to be with a narcissist. We constantly receive mixed messages from them and can't seem to wrap our heads around this mystery.

They may be in a fantastic mood while you're at a dinner party with your friends. They may shower you with compliments and treat you to a dance. But the love is gone as soon as you return home. The compliments are left at the dinner table and you, in turn, are left wondering what happened. Often, we dismiss their two-faced nature as "tough love" in an attempt to explain the inexplicable. Sometimes we romanticise peaceful and pleasant moments in an otherwise abusive and painful relationship due to media influence or our longing for happiness. In fact, the short moments of peace and happiness in an otherwise unhealthy relationship give us a reason to hold on to it. Narcissists are quick to point out the good things they've done for us in an argument, as if the good things cancel out the bad. You must never be expected to put up with abusive behaviour in a relationship just because you receive hugs and kisses for Christmas and gifts on your birthday.

Every relationship goes through hard times, but the key to a sustainable, mutually beneficial partnership lies in teamwork. A healthy relationship consists of two or more people working together to build a strong foundation of love and respect for each other, despite all the differences. Thus, the previously mentioned examples can be applied to romantic and family relationships alike.

It is important to understand that a truly confident person doesn't need to put on a show for anyone. Someone with a high level of confidence also doesn't need to put other people down in order to make themselves feel better. In life, you can either lift people up or pull people down depending on where you're at, emotionally. Someone with a healthy level of self-esteem will not easily be affected by another person's judgment or criticism. He or she will not be preoccupied with impressing others to the degree where they seem to have a split personality.

In reality, a narcissist is just as concerned with themselves as they are concerned with what other people think about them. The biggest fear of a narcissist is to look bad in front of other people. The reason behind looking attractive, owning a nice car and faking a perfect family life in front of others is not that the narcissist "fell in love with themselves" - narcissists want others to fall in love with them. Think about the time before you got seriously involved with the narcissist in your life. There is a high chance you also thought that he or she was such a charming person in the same way your friends, family and colleagues may still think about them now.

Narcissists have a fragile sense of identity. It might have gotten damaged through heavy trauma when they were young adults, or their sense of identity never fully formed when they were children due to previously discussed reasons. The result is a weak sense of identity which also comes with lifelong low levels of self-esteem. After all, if you don't have a stable sense of who you are (identity), then how could you truly value yourself (self-esteem)? Because of these feelings of lack, narcissists try to build their identity around the thoughts they project on others. They don't feel to be "enough" by themselves, so they try to control and take away from others in order to fill in the gaps and build themselves up. If they want a person to admire them, they will make sure to elicit admiration from the targeted individual in one way or another.

Dealing with Low Self-Esteem

As a narcissist likely raised by a house that was not understanding of narcissists, your belief system has probably been wired in a way that reduced your self-esteem. Because you were not well-understood growing up, a lot of the beliefs you gained from family, friends, and society itself may have insinuated that you were "broken" and that you needed fixing. In other words, they did not understand you, they were intimidated by your differences, and they wanted to break you down and make you more "normal." This can lead to low self-esteem as a result of not feeling confident in your ability to express yourself as who you are. You may have even learned to express yourself in a way that is not accurate to who you truly are, causing you to feel dissociated from your own identity. If this happened in adolescence when you were in the process of discovering your identity, this could be particularly damaging to your self-esteem.

The best way to regain your self-esteem and increase your confidence levels can be done through a number of ways. The first step is becoming aware of your truth and knowing who you are. If you have made it this far into the book, you have already made step one. If you are just discovering this information for the first time it may take a while to sink in, but once you have developed an understanding of who you are, you can begin to make sense of everything (including your past) and progress to the next steps to improving your self-esteem and becoming a confident narcissist.

DO NOT OBSESS

One of the first steps in rewiring yourself is unwiring every negative belief you have picked up throughout your life. This means disassembling your belief systems and replacing them with true, empowering beliefs. This is not an easy task and takes time replacing old beliefs with more empowering beliefs. Once accomplished, it allows you to step into a better reality and live life from your own perspective, as opposed to living a life with clouded judgments influenced by other people's negative beliefs.

To begin the unwiring process, challenge, and question everything. Every time you begin behaving as a result of a specific belief you have, question it. Ask yourself where that belief came from and if it truly is yours. If not, begin the process of replacing the old negative belief with your true empowering belief by first identifying the new belief, then reinforcing it by using positive affirmations, visualisation, and goal setting.

It is important to understand that when you are in the process of unwiring your beliefs to later rewire them with your true beliefs, you must make sure that you are not choosing your beliefs based on popular thinking or opinion. You are your own person, and you are entitled to have your own beliefs, even if they are against popular opinion. Unpopular beliefs are a reality of life and, when they are being honest, virtually everyone will admit that they have a handful of unpopular beliefs. Just because we do not tend to talk about them as often does not mean they still exist. Use your intuition when choosing what beliefs to instill. The beliefs that resonate with you and make you feel aligned to who you are will be the most beneficial.

It is important that you do not endure the entire unwiring and rewiring process only to find yourself coming out the other side with more beliefs that are not true to who you are. This can be a challenge, especially if you are facing low self-esteem and low self-confidence from your conditioning and upbringing, but it is important. Take your time and make sure that as you undergo this process, you also give yourself the space to heal. Healing each layer as you peel it back is an important part of the process. As you heal, you give yourself permission to fully unwire and release all of these negative beliefs and replace them with your own true empowering beliefs, popularity aside.

As you continue to go through this process, you will likely find that there are far more beliefs to be replaced than you initially thought there would be. Since you are a narcissist, you have been absorbing beliefs your entire life, whether they were yours or not. Let yourself release them so that in their place you can input your true beliefs, thus giving you freedom from the false negative beliefs you have been holding onto and allowing you to live a life aligned with your true positive beliefs that serve you.

Positive beliefs and intentions are any beliefs and intentions that genuinely align with your best interest. These positive beliefs and intentions can often be contradicted by uninspiring, negative beliefs you have been fed growing up.

When you are in the process of rewiring, make sure that the beliefs you are rewiring with are positive and genuinely serve your wellbeing and the wellbeing of others, as well. You can do this by taking a few moments to consider each new belief that you want to affirm to yourself and implant within you. For example, you may have the belief, "money is bad because it makes people evil" which is not a very empowering or positive belief system. Instead, you may want to reframe your perspective and create a new belief, "I will be wealthy and I choose to be loving in how I use my money."

Now, obviously it is going to take some time to replace the old belief with a more empowering positive belief. To achieve full replacement with the new belief, it needs to be ingrained into your subconscious mind. That is how the positive belief will actually have an effect on your life.

In order to ingrain the new empowering, positive belief into your subconscious mind, you will need to use the power of repetition. This is what the subconscious mind responds to. Once something has been repeated enough times, it will become "automatic" or in this case "subconscious."

Learn how to ground

Grounding is another effective way to cleanse yourself of negative energy. Another important feature of this technique, which, unfortunately, is left ignored is having a good connection with

Mother Earth. When you do "grounding," you connect with the Earth and cleanse yourself off all negative energy. The steps are as follows:

- ☐ Assume a sitting or lying position. The important thing is to keep your feet flat on the ground. It is recommended that you try this exercise with your bare feet touching the soil or grass. However, if this is not possible, simply keep your feet flat on the ground. Just relax and feel the Earth beneath your feet.

- ☐ Breathe in and out gently. Now, visualise roots from your feet extending down deep into the Earth. Do not force it. Just allow it to extend comfortably. Allow it to stop naturally. Now, feel your connection to Mother Earth.

- ☐ Inhale slowly, and as you exhale, see and feel that you also exhale all the negative energy in your body.

- ☐ Exhale it through your roots. Visualise it as something black that flows down your roots and into the Earth. Do not worry, the Earth is very powerful, and all the negative energy that you send to the Earth shall be neutralised. If you want, you can also breathe in positive energy.

- ☐ The way to do this is to visualise the green energy of the Earth as you inhale. Allow it to flow through your roots and enter your body via the soles of your feet. As you do this exercise, feel and appreciate the wonderful connection that you have with Mother Earth.

This technique is very effective when you want to cleanse yourself and release negative energy, as well as for charging yourself with the

Earth's positive energy. Once you get good at using this technique, you can use it even in public.

There are also other ways to ground. If you want, you can use your hands instead of your feet. Another easy way to ground is by hugging a tree, preferably a big one, and feel just how connected you are to it. When you are afraid, it is a good practice to ground yourself and find strength as you are connected to the Earth. You should realise that you have always been close to the Earth. From the time you were born, you have been swimming in the Earth's energy. By connecting to the Earth, not only can you release negative energy, but you can also empower yourself and fill yourself with positive energy.

POSITIVE VISUALIZATION

You might not have experienced it yet, but narcissists have great potential to be creative. Positive Visualisation can be a great way to use that creativity you contain and is also a great tool to support your mind in genuinely being able to see a positive future. It gets your mind working and starts the manifestation process. Imagine the ideal situation you'd like to be in a few years from now. Where is that place for you? What does it sound like? Who are the people around you? What do you look like? How do you feel? What luxuries are there? For many, visualising positive things happening for them is a challenge. If you can begin to practice incorporating positive visualisation into your daily life, it becomes easier and easier for you to see, believe and work towards what you desire to have. Then, it becomes easier for you to actually have it. Pick a time of the day that best suits you to do some positive visualisation.

POSITIVE AFFIRMATIONS

Positive Affirmations are a great tool to add to visualisation because they support you in having a positive, can-do attitude toward achieving your goals. It can be very powerful to start writing, reciting and listening to positive affirmations of things you would like to be or have in your life. When repeated on a daily basis, it will start to mould your mind and perspective towards positivity. Examples of some empowering positive affirmations include: I have the power to create change

- ☐ I forgive myself for my past
- ☐ I am a creative being
- ☐ Positivity is a choice I choose to make everyday
- ☐ I choose to be happy and completely love myself today
- ☐ I am becoming a better version of myself each and everyday
- ☐ Beautiful things happen to me
- ☐ I do not seek approval from anyone. I am enough
- ☐ I only surround myself with positive and encouraging people
- ☐ I am deserving of an abundant lifestyle
- ☐ I am successful
- ☐ I take responsibility for my successes and failures
- ☐ I will accept nothing but the best
- ☐ New opportunities come easily to me
- ☐ Positive energy surrounds me
- ☐ I set clear goals and work to complete them everyday

GOAL SETTING

Goal Setting is incredibly important because it takes your dreams and desires into account and gives you a real focus toward achieving them and bringing them into your reality. There is something incredibly powerful about writing down your goals. By writing a goal down that you want to achieve in the future allows the goal to become more real in the mind. Once the goal has been written down it becomes easier to break the goal down into smaller goals in order to achieve the desired goal. Another benefit of writing down your goals is it allows you to be reminded of the goal every day and remain focused. Something like a whiteboard can be a great addition to your bedroom so you can see your goals every day when you wake up. Add some pictures or photos next to these goals for more motivation. Make it become more real in the mind.

APPRECIATION AND GRATITUDE JOURNALS

This particular tool, Appreciation and Gratitude Journals are a great tool to pause and reflect on the present moment and recognise all the things you are grateful for. It can become very easy to get caught up in the future which can leave us unsatisfied at times because we are always wanting more. It's important to stop and take the time to appreciate what we have in life.

The powerful thing about taking the time to recognise what you are appreciative for and writing this down in your gratitude journal, is that you actually increase your vibration and you will naturally attract more things in the future to be grateful for. Crazy right?

It can also be an effective method to shift your perspective when you feel like you 'have the world on your shoulders' and things aren't actually that bad.

All of these five tools will work best collectively to encourage you, motivate you, give you hope, improve your self-esteem, and inspire you to keep pushing in a positive direction.

CONSUMING POSITIVE SELF-DEVELOPMENT MATERIAL

Another great way to rewire your brain is to continually consume positive self-development material. Reading and listening to materials that are designed to inform you about new perspectives, share opinions with you, and support you in rewiring your brain to a more positive mindset are all extremely powerful in unwiring your brain from negative conditioning you received growing up.

It will be especially beneficial if you consume content that is specific to Empaths, as they will be more mindful of how you actually experience the world around you. This type of material can serve you by educating your mind and rewiring your subconscious to let go of beliefs that no longer serve you and replace them with beliefs that will empower you, build your self-esteem and self-confidence, and support you in using your Empathic gift for wonderful things.

Get Away from the Noise – Live by Yourself

When you are seeking to rewire your brain, it is important to give yourself the space to discover who you truly are and learn what you want to learn. One of the best ways of doing this is living on your own at least for a while. This gives you a chance to be completely alone and experience who you truly are, free of the pressure of anyone else in your life. It is also a great way to rid yourself of any bad, negative energy that you might have been absorbing.

If you are unable to live alone because you already have a family or you are under conditions where you have to live with other people, consider spending a significant amount of time on your own. Schedule regular breaks and times to be completely by yourself. While this won't be exactly the same, it will give you the opportunity to hear yourself think and figure out what you like to do when you are by yourself. This can support you in having a deeper understanding of who you are, and therefore a greater confidence in expressing yourself.

Even if you can travel somewhere for a period of time by yourself, I would highly recommend this. Get away from the noise and hear yourself think. Take the time to reflect.

Putting Yourself First

Narcissists are known for struggling to put themselves first, no matter what the situation is. Many will continue to put others first even long after they begin paying the physical, mental, and emotional price for this behaviour. This is a significant symptom of the wounded healer.

Putting yourself first is one of the most selfless things you can do. If you truly want to support other people, putting yourself first and taking care of yourself with the highest quality of care and compassion will support you in being mentally, emotionally, and physically available to support yourself and others for a long time. Treasure yourself in every way possible, and always put yourself first. Be willing to say no, and practice setting boundaries, so that you do not deplete your own energy in favour of someone else's needs. Stop tolerating bad energy and negative people.

Surrounding Yourself with The Right Energy

If you are spending time around people with negative energy and are regularly reinforcing negative beliefs around you, you are going to feel an integration of negative energy and beliefs in your own life. Even the most experienced narcissists who have been masterfully protecting themselves and their energy for years find themselves adopting the negative energy and beliefs of those they are around, especially on a regular basis. With narcissists, the people we are emotionally close to seem to have the ability to penetrate through our protection. Although we can work harder to create protection that is impenetrable, consistent exposure can lead to "leaks." Think of it like having constant pressure on the other side of your bubble. Eventually, no matter how hard you try, the bubble can and will burst. If you spend too much time around negative energy and negative beliefs, it will affect you no matter what. It is best to focus on surrounding yourself with the right positive energy rather than trying to fight the negative energy.

Spending majority of your time around people who you can share a positive and healthy relationship with is very important. This does not necessarily mean that you need to discard your old friends and those who you hung out with most. Rather, it simply means spending less time with them in favour of spending more time with people who help you feel great. When you spend time with people who have a positive energy and a set of positive beliefs, you begin to foster these in the same way that you would with negative energy and beliefs. This means that you can begin to experience greater joy in your life. For many narcissists, surrounding themselves with the right group of friends can feel like they are finally coming home to the family they always wanted. It can truly be life changing.

Chapter 5: The Nature of Narcissistic Personality Disorder

As modern culture is defined by the rise of social media, YouTube and reality TV stardom, dating through phone applications, and individuals struggling to find self-worth in a global internet age, narcissism has become a hot topic on multiple fronts. Most of us think of Narcissistic Personality Disorder as an extreme form of arrogance, or an inclination towards conceited behaviours. With so many people competing for five seconds of fame, recognition, or even just attention, we could easily see it as a widespread epidemic, vilify it, and blame it for everything that's wrong with our society today.

In truth, Narcissistic Personality Disorder is quite widespread, though it's hardly an epidemic. We all have it, to some degree, and for most of us, it's a tool that helps to keep us physically and mentally healthy, rather than a destructive, negative characteristic. Narcissistic impulse is what compels most of us to take care of our bodies, even when it's inconvenient; to rest, even if there is more work to be done; to eat enough to satiate our own hunger, despite the fact that somewhere on the planet, children are starving. It's what allows you to say "no," when saying "yes" might push you beyond your limits, and it's a big part of what stops you from hurting or killing yourself every time you feel sad.

It can be helpful to think of NPD in the same terms that we use to discuss food addiction. I reference food rather than alcohol or drug addiction because food addicts do not have the option of total abstinence; in order to manage their addictions, they must grow comfortable with regularly dipping their toes in the water, sometimes wading, but never diving in. Narcissism is similar; it is not a disease, nor is it something we should seek to eradicate entirely from our psyches, but when it becomes our sole focus or primary drive, we can become a danger to others and to ourselves. Much like a food addict, in order to heal, a narcissist wouldn't just need to alter their behaviours; they would also need to engage in deep self-reflection and try to find the emotional root of their disordered thinking. Sadly, this is something most narcissists would never volunteer themselves to do.

To be diagnosed with NPD, one must display a severe lack of emotional empathy. While the average person can embrace narcissistic attitudes from time to time, a true narcissist suffers from a deeply distorted view of the self and the world around them. Reality checks are no match for their twisted, warped thought processes. In the narcissist's mind, they are the most important and admirable person around, no matter where they go, and since they don't empathise with other people, they believe it's rational to assume that most others agree with them. They expect preferential treatment and special recognition, even if they haven't worked to earn it. They talk down to others without remorse and exhibit grandiose behaviours to assert their superiority. Most worryingly, they avoid honest self-reflection, guilt, and shame at all costs, so their minds become well-practiced at rewriting truths, delusionary thinking, denial, rationalising the illogical, and justifying their morally bankrupt decisions.

Narcissistic Personality Disorder is a fluid trait, like shyness or generosity. It's natural for people to go through temporary phases of heightened narcissism, particularly after an achievement or instance of special recognition, or, alternatively, many people with healthy minds can lean further into their narcissistic impulses after being rejected or disparaged. So long as the attitudes have a temporary effect on mindset and behaviour, both reactions are perfectly normal and healthy. Narcissistic Personality Disorder isn't always bad, corrosive, destructive, or permanent; in some situations, in fact, it is necessary. Many people are explicitly and obnoxiously narcissistic in adolescence, though most outgrow the trait by early adulthood; some would argue that this attitude shift is integral in a teenager's development, urging them towards independence from their family unit. For another example, an individual might purposefully strive to become more narcissistic after leaving an abusive relationship dynamic wherein their self-worth was diminished. In this case, narcissism is needed to foster healing, inspire growth, and develop personal agency. At its core, narcissism is a survival instinct.

It is not the mere existence of narcissistic impulse that ails these people; it's the fact that their narcissism has become paramount, distorting their perceptions of reality and corrupting rationality. Many recovering alcoholics will say that they didn't consume alcohol to feel intoxicated, but instead drank to try and fill a bottomless emotional hole; similarly, a diagnosed narcissist's need for attention and markers of superiority can be compulsive, obsessive, and relentless. A true narcissist will never reach a point wherein they are satisfied with their accomplishments or the degree of power they hold, nor will they ever feel conflicted about the lengths to which they'll go to satisfy their own ego.

This disorder has an effect on the everyday life of those that are suffering from it and its effects are always on the negative side. Generally, narcissists tend to be very unhappy with life and whenever they find that people are not giving them the attention and admiration they desire, they get disappointed. Although they may not acknowledge their role in the downturn of their personal relationships or work, the fact remains that these aspects of their lives suffer, and they may not realise the damage they are causing themselves and others.

Other people may find it easy to run away from those that are suffering from this condition because they may not enjoy being around them, which contributes to the narcissist's feeling of being unfulfilled at home, work and in their social lives.

Narcissists come in all shapes and sizes. They can be male, female, gender fluid or non-binary; they can be wealthy, middle class, or impoverished; they can be young or old; they can be single, committed to monogamy, or polyamorous love; they can be highly educated or hardly educated at all. They can be of any race, culture, or religious faith.

Some of them are easy to spot from a distance, but some can fly under the radar, seeming fairly well-adjusted at first glance. While the specifics of their personae can vary widely, there are some behavioural traits that are commonly found in narcissists of all kinds. These are behaviours or attitudes that some of us occasionally exhibit, perhaps as a reaction to rejection or grief, or when we are overwhelmed by stress.

Even licensed therapists aren't able to make diagnoses of NPD based on observation alone, and if the person in question isn't a family member or spouse, chances are you haven't had the time or opportunity to examine their behaviour from all angles. You have your own life, after all, and hopefully plenty of personal concerns that distract you from analysing the behaviours of other people in depth.

Sometimes, though, a diagnosis isn't the goal. You may have purchased this book because you suspect another person's narcissism is impacting your life or your mindset through the relationship you share with them. If this is the case, it isn't important to get a diagnosis for them, or even hope that they'll change through treatment. What's important is that you recognise the abusive relationship dynamic for what it is, and take whatever steps are necessary to protect your emotional and physical health.

Chapter 6: Narcissistic scale

Is This You?

Below you can find a set of sentences that perfectly describe how narcissists view themselves and how they relate to others:

- ☐ I love myself, and I am certain you do too. I cannot imagine anyone not loving me!

- ☐ I don't have to apologise. However, you must not only understand and accept, but you must also tolerate everything that I say and do.

- ☐ I don't think I have any equals in this world; if so, I have yet to meet one. I am the best (student, partner, businessman, parent, etc.).

- ☐ If I am not there to offer guidance and leadership, others will be lost.

- ☐ I understand that there are certain rules and duties, but they apply to you and not to me. I neither have the time nor the inclination to follow such rules. Also, rules are only for regular people, and I am certainly quite special.

- ☐ I hope you understand and appreciate all that I have achieved for you and all that I am because I am perfect and delightful.

- ☐ I do wish that we were equals, but we aren't, and we can never be. I will keep reminding you constantly that I am the most brilliant person in the room and am successful in all different aspects of life. You need to be grateful for my success.

- [ ] I might seem arrogant or haughty, and it is fine with me. I don't ever want to seem like an average person.

- [ ] I always expect you to be loyal to me, regardless of what I do. However, it is unfair if you expect the same from me.

- [ ] I am not manipulative; I like it when things go according to my wishes, regardless of all the trouble it causes you or others. I am not concerned with how others feel. In fact, I believe that feelings are only meant for the weak.

- [ ] I expect your gratitude, and I always expect you to be grateful for all that I do, even the smallest of deeds. I also expect you to do as I say.

- [ ] I only like to associate myself with those who are exemplary. I believe that most of my friends can never measure up.

- [ ] Things will be so much better if you do as I say, no questions asked.

- [ ] As you can imagine, it is rather difficult to live or work with someone who behaves in this manner.

For many people, discovering a new label for how you identify and who you are can be both scary and liberating. On one hand, you have a new term for who and what you are. This means that you are now "diagnosed" as a certain type of person. However, it also means that you are now able to discover more about yourself. Having a label for who and what you are opens up the opportunity to learn what that means and how it impacts you in your life. As a result, it can be liberating to know that you are not alone and that there are ways for you to create a powerful and enjoyable life with your new label in tow.

Like all other labels, identifying if you are a narcissist is not entirely by choice. Rather, you either are a narcissist, or you aren't one. Then, you can choose whether or not you want to use the identity. Of course, you can abandon the identity and deny who you are. Or, you can embody it and embrace the reality that you are a narcissist, and you can begin using great strategies and tools to thrive in life, rather than to live in fear.

Still, before you embody the new label, you really want to make sure that you completely identify. Knowing for certain is essential as it helps us embody who we are and feel more complete in our identity. So, I want you to take a read through the narcissist Checklist and see if you can relate to that.

Here are the questions to answer honestly to determine if your narcissism is getting past the point of normally healthy self-love and respect.

Narcissist Checklist

- ☐ Can you be generous without being recognised?
- ☐ Can you actually put the needs of someone else ahead of your own?
- ☐ Are you capable of listening?
- ☐ Can you take any kind of criticism?

How do you score yourself?

If you have done even one of these things, you have behaved badly. It might have been a lapse in judgment and you may have felt bad afterwards and determined to be more sensitive and mature in the future.

But if you have recognised yourself in two or more of these scenarios, you are exhibiting narcissistic behaviour. If you or some aspect of you is visible in all of them, your behaviour is seriously narcissistic and you need to consider some kind of intervention or therapy.

You can help yourself unless you are in the seriously advanced stages of narcissism and need professional therapy.

For the average narcissist, however, recognising your tendency to think only of yourself is a good square one.

You didn't develop those unpleasant behaviours overnight and you won't be able to just snap your fingers and get rid of them.

But you will be able to set out a course of small steps to move you back to more normally accepted behaviour that will enrich your life and the lives of those around you.

If you relate to the above scenario, then there is a good chance that you are a narcissist. Many narcissists are diagnosed with anxiety and depressive disorders because of how they experience the world around them. Being a narcissist does not mean that you do not actually possess these disorders. Rather, it means that you may now have a reason as to why.

If most of these sounded very familiar to you and you checked most of the statements above, then you can be pretty confident that you are a narcissist.

For that reason, it's a good idea to make sure that you begin practicing these protection and self-care practices as soon as possible and that you really integrate them into your life. The more you practice and use them, the easier it will become to rely on them and have trust in them. Then, they will begin to support you in having a happier and healthier life that is less overwhelming and isolating.

Chapter 7: The Child That Didn't Emotionally Grow Up

Children growing up with narcissistic parents often feel like their young worlds are imploding. They will often feel like they are not seen, invisible to their parent or parents; like they will never be heard or be considered; they will feel like they are simply an item that just belongs to their parent; and that they will never be acknowledged. This has a mental effect on a child that begins to develop and then constantly develops and grows and transforms until that child is suffering with feelings of distrust, identity, a high level of anxiety, and possibly depression. The child is exposed to lies and inhibitions of their parent that can change that child's way of thinking, a sudden maturity brought on by a lack of responsible parenting. That can only have negative effects on that child and nothing more. But this emotional maturity can also be stunted, stopped, due to the unfortunate calamity of having a childhood besotted by bad memories. The child will feel as if the walls close in fast and that they have not been nurtured as a child should be when that child sees how other parents interact with their children. That brings with it a sense of not being good enough, a feeling of needing to do more for their parent or parents to receive that praise they long for and deserve. The child feels as if they need to change, they feel it is because of them that their parent, or parents, is not giving them the time of day to be seen, heard, embraced. They feel used, and thus end up harbouring guilt-infused confusion. They grow up feeling lost, walking around with such anxiety which has now consumed them and defines them. It is tragic that these children have to suffer through this; that they have to grow up feeling like the world is just going to use them too. They lack self-esteem. They don't seek validation for who they are but what they look like because their parent or parents constantly picked away at them and at their image. They become self-conscious adults who have to hit reset and seek help and to find their clarity again.

Effects of Being Raised by Narcissists

It can be difficult to foretell how somebody raised by narcissists will react. Psychology is an extremely fickle beast, and there is no certain path for anything. This sad reality provides the basis for most psychological ends. However, people who are raised by narcissists will generally see the effects manifest in either one of two ways.

Generally, if somebody is raised by narcissists, either they will respond *reactively,* or they will respond *abidingly.* Both have two extremely different psychological outcomes in regards to the individual, but they can nonetheless yield a very interesting insight into the post-adolescent mindset of people who have been raised by narcissists.

First, we're going to discuss what happens when somebody responds *abidingly* to their narcissistic parents. This is, unfortunately, the most common reaction, and the most serious one.

The sad thing about genetics and environment is that both of these can have an effect on a given person's predisposition to environmental change. Studies have shown that more reserved and conservative individuals usually come from stricter or more generally hostile environments. Therefore, their radically submissive personality comes largely as a subconscious reaction to the stimuli of these environments.

Abiding reactions start by never having the will to question your parents. If they say they are the best, or that they are the absolute greatest, the abiding reaction is to take what they say as fact. This is rooted in a child's innate reverence of their parental figures and later reinforced by the continued mental and psychological trauma inflicted by the abusive narcissistic parent.

It's not uncommon for somebody with narcissistic parents to be constantly controlled – think of the *helicopter parent* type, but doing so only out of their own self-interest rather than an obsession with the interests of their child – and also constantly degraded or told that they aren't doing well enough or simply aren't up to snuff in their narcissistic parent's eyes. Acting counter to this will often be met with aggression on the end of the narcissistic parent. People with a narcissistic personality disorder will often also display an inability to tolerate criticism, so any criticism by their child will be taken very harshly.

This reaction is, unfortunately, more common than it might seem. It'll start to affect your personal relationships with other people if you develop it to the extent that you can't empathise with other people or you drive them away through your narcissistic tendencies. The best way to deal with it at this point is to accept that your parents are not godlike figures. They are fallible, and they likely have caused a lot of mental trauma that you can't accept.

The long-term, lasting effects of abiding reaction are difficult to really deal with. They come from developing a sense of self-awareness and knowing both *what you are worth* and what you *aren't* worth. At the root of narcissistic personality disorder is an incredibly fragile ego that's bolstered by an irrational and delusional sense of self. The narcissist has an incredibly hard time knowing their genuine worth. Unsurprisingly, narcissism is often associated with other disorders such as bipolar disorder, major depression, or any number of anxiety disorders - all of which can lead to the development of narcissism as a coping mechanism.

It's worth making the personal assessment to determine whether or not you may have developed narcissistic qualities yourself. How do you treat others? How do you project yourself? How do you *define* yourself? Your answers to these questions are all intrinsic behavioural definitions that have a huge impact on your overall psyche and the way you present yourself to others.

You also need to spend time learning about manipulation tactics and learn about what things you may have picked up unwittingly. The unfortunate truth is that many people who are raised by narcissists do tend to have very meek views of themselves. People who are narcissists will more often than not degrade the people around them to make them feel better about themselves. The long-lasting mental implications of being constantly degraded are numerous and all entirely negative. Depending on the nature of the insults, it can cause reactions such as social anxiety disorder, body dysphoria, and any number of related issues.

Many of these issues will never be addressed unless the person who has been affected by a narcissistic parent takes the steps to heal properly. The healing process may either be simple or complicated, but either way, they are absolutely essential in the long term.

A person who reacts reactively may feel bizarre for having resentment towards their parents or may feel as though they're just overreacting. This could be reinforced if the parent gaslights their child in response to criticism by simply overreacting, invalidating their opinions or even calling them crazy.

The good news is that when somebody is reacting reactively and pushing back against their parents, their long-term success rates in terms of building a healthy life after being raised by a narcissistic parent are much higher than someone who simply internalises the actions of their narcissistic parent as normal and indeed develops many of the traits for themselves. They have a much better rate of self-normalisation,< and tend to have far more stable relationships throughout their life.

If you have a creeping suspicion that you were raised by narcissists, then you've already taken the first step which is so important: realising that your parents are not perfect beings and that they can make mistakes and, more importantly, that their mistakes can have a negative effect on your emotional wellbeing. Taking that step is the most difficult part. Sure, everything else seems hard, but it takes so much courage to recognise that there could be an issue with your parents and I really commend you for doing so.

Children of narcissistic parents often remain unaware of the parent's personality disorder until they reach adulthood themselves; in fact, some are unable to come to terms with this truth until very late in life, long after the narcissistic parent is deceased. It's easy to understand how a child's view of their own parent can be deeply and almost irreversibly warped by narcissistic attitudes; at a young age, children don't realise that they can question the parent's behaviour, or even examine it with a critical eye, and the narcissistic parent has total and absolute control over the relationship dynamics within their household. Typically, the child's needs are underserved, with the majority of the emotional energy in the household directed towards keeping the narcissist satisfied, whatever the cost.

Chapter 8: Empathy can be learned

A lack of empathy is one of the most prominent emotional issues associated with narcissism. Those without narcissism generally have at least some empathy naturally. It is also possible to learn to become a more empathetic person. Empathy is simply defined as the ability to share in and understand the feelings of others. A narcissist has no empathy and no ability to just try and develop it. In fact, they do not understand it and have no use for it. When someone around them is showing empathy to another person, this can actually make the narcissist feel angry since all of the attention is not on them.

Every person already has some level of empathy. From this point of view, it can be said that everyone is an empath. However, those who are properly called as "empaths" are those who have much higher sensitivity than the usual. So, just to answer the question, yes empathy can be learned and developed. The techniques and practices in this book will help you learn and develop your empathic ability. However, it should be noted that acquiring knowledge alone is not enough to take control of your ability. You also need to engage in the actual and continuous practice to learn the techniques in this book.

Empathy is defined as the ability to easily sense and feel other people's feelings or emotions. It's characterised by a heightened sensitivity to such emotions. However, it should be noted that empathy means more than just being able to sense emotions. More specifically, it is about being sensitive and being able to feel the subtle energy. It should be noted that everything is made of energy, even conventional science has proven this as a fact.

When you have empathy, then you do not perceive the world as most other people do. You get to immerse yourself in a world that is rich in emotions and feelings. Unfortunately, these emotions in the form of energy can be problematic, especially if you do not know how to control and use your ability properly. It's also worth noting that every person has some level of empathy. There are simply some people who are more sensitive than others.

You need to learn to be in control of your ability instead of the other way around. Unfortunately, many empaths end up being controlled by other people's emotions. What makes this worse is that they tend to attract negative energies instead of positive ones. If you attract and get connected with negative energies, then you will soon end up being negative yourself. You have to learn to deal with various emotions and energies. Once you can finally control your ability, then you will soon realise how helpful it can be. Yes, you can help people, including yourself, with empathy. This ability will allow you to connect and understand people on a deeper and more meaningful way. As such, it can help give you a life full of love, peace, and happiness. Listen: You have a gift. You simply have to learn to use it as one.

Do you feel drained after being with people? This is a common signal that you probably have empathy. It usually happens after interacting with people, especially when you interact with negative people. Many times, even without interaction, but just the mere presence of other people can make you feel drained. You might notice this when you go to populated places like the mall. The reason why this happens will be discussed later in the book. This can also happen when you interact with a negative person. If you often have this kind of experience, then it is a usual sign of empathy.

Do you have a need to have alone-time for yourself? If you feel like you need to take a step back from people and only spend time with yourself, then you are probably an empath. Empaths normally need to be alone from time to time, especially as a way to release tension and stress.

Being too exposed to people can expose you to various energies, and this can be chaotic in the long run. Hence, having a time of solitude is needed.

The main thing that characterises an empath is their oversensitivity. If you are oversensitive, such as being easily offended, or if you appreciate things easily, then such level of sensitivity normally shows empathy.

Chapter 9: Develop and Deliver Substance

By the process of both recognising and separating themselves from their inner voices of self-soothing, self-aggrandizing and self-attacking, narcissists can indeed overcome this terrible state of mind that also classifies as a mental disorder. This is no easy task, but it has been seen and done successfully. The attitudes they internalised and have utilised from early childhood are deeply intertwined within them. But one of the best methods of conquering narcissism is the process of voice therapy.

Voice therapy is a very powerful technique that is able to tap onto a person's negative core beliefs. It identifies negative thought patterns that are in control of the individual's narcissistic behaviour. The process of switching the verbalisations into a second person point of view allow the narcissist to separate their own points of view from the hostile point of view back onto themselves. It allows them to receive a taste of their own medicine, in other words. Narcissists also need to learn to differentiate the traits that their parents or caretakers still act upon to this day. Being around that behaviour only drives them to think they can continue it without too much consequence. This also goes for the adaptations they had to make when their parents neglected them growing up. To be able to break the patterns of their self-centred behaviours, they must do these vital things to be able to get to a path to begin to tread upon. Fighting the urge to compare themselves to the likes of others, as well as the need to be the best and the most perfect all the time is one of the aspects of being a narcissist that is the hardest to overcome.

The process of fostering self-compassion rather than self-esteem is another practice that many have seen success in when it comes to curing narcissists and their behaviours. Self-esteem centres itself on the evaluation of oneself in relation to others, while self-compassion focuses on treating yourself with kindness, recognising the shared qualities of you versus the rest of humanity, as well as being mindful when pondering over negative aspects of yourself. Studies have actually found that focusing on raining self-esteem actually worsens narcissistic actions and behaviours, as raising awareness of self-compassion combats it. This is because it includes the idea of a shared humanity with other people, leading to thinking about others before oneself.

The process of developing transcendent goals, taking the time to truly invest and care about other people is another hard to do but crucial way to cure narcissism. Having opportunities to be generous to others should be highly sought out for those that want to change their narcissistic ways of life. Living within these corrective opportunities that come to light intensely assist the build of a real, intact self-esteem and practice focusing on others rather than sustaining all of one's energy within themselves only.

Four tips to remember when you start your trek to overcoming your narcissistic ways:

- ☐ **Empathy** – attempt to put yourself within the shoes of other people. Taking a look at the real world and realising other people have it tougher than you can get you to take less focus off yourself and your issues and help out others if they need it.

- **Open to Criticism** – learn to be polite when you do not like the opinions of other people about yourself or things you do. Do not be close-minded to what others have to think all the time.

- **Learn to Laugh at Yourself** – do not beat yourself up if you do not end up living to your own expectations. You are not perfect, and everyone makes mistakes. Laugh at yourself and know you can do better next time.

- **Don't Always Have the Mindset of a Competitor** – bragging about everything you have achieved and accomplished is not something people want to hear about 24/7. Learn to remain modest in your successes.

If none of the above techniques do the trick, there is always professional treatment. Getting to the point of recognising your behaviours and wanting to change them is a big step! With the help of patience, courage and a true commitment to you, therapy is a great option. Therapists can provide boundaries that narcissists would otherwise refuse from their spouses or significant others. With the increase of self-acceptance, processes of psychotherapy have been shown and proven to greatly increase the positive aspects of a narcissist's way of life and quality of living.

Understanding your fears

It is also important for you to understand your fears. First, you need to identify them. After identifying your fears, you need to understand them. What causes your fears? Are there good reasons for your fears? Once you are able to identify your fears, you can now take positive actions to resolve them. Take note that it is okay to have fears. A common mistake is not to admit your fears. If you don't recognise them, then there is no way that you can face and overcome them.

Think about what evokes your fear? Is it the fear of not being accepted by others? There are no hard and fast rules on this. You really need to take the time to reflect and understand what your fears are. Again, it is important that you start to recognise them. You should also consider the effects of your fear. Do not be surprised if you find some of the things that you fear to be groundless or something that you should not fear at all. Indeed, many of the things that people fear come from mere misunderstanding. However, if you move and look closer at what you fear, there is a good chance that you see find that there is no good reason to fear it at all. The more that you understand your fear, the more that you can identify the right actions that you should take to overcome it.

Self-acceptance and realisation

Before others can accept you, you first need to accept yourself. A part of this is accepting your ability. Keep in mind that your empathic ability is a gift, as long as you use it properly. Accept who you are as a person, including your weaknesses, and learn to love yourself. Now, it should be noted that recognising your weaknesses does not mean that you will not do anything about them. Instead, you should accept your imperfections but still do your best to correct them. There is simply no end to self-improvement.

It is important to note that this acceptance should be made peacefully. If you cannot do it in peace, then it only means that there is still something about you that you do not fully understand. More importantly, you should learn to accept your gift. Yes, it may be hard in the beginning. But, once you learn how to use it properly, only then you will realise that empathy is indeed a gift, and it is something that you can use to help people, including yourself.

You vs. the world

If you have come up with the right realisation, then you should know that you don't have to go against the world. In fact, the world can be a beautiful place for you to live in. Just as you accept other people with their flaws and imperfections, you should also accept yourself. When you do this, other people will also be able to accept you for who you are. Acceptance begins with yourself.

Do not allow your ability to hinder you from connecting with other people. You should realise that love, happiness, peace, and kindness – all these things need you to be with another person. If you just shut your doors from everyone, then you will end up alone facing life all by yourself. However, you should remember that you have a choice. By practicing the techniques in this book, you can mingle and socialise with people and fill your life with happiness, love, and peace. The world is not your enemy. You only need to conquer yourself.

Chapter 10: Effects on Everyday Life and How to Live with the Disorder

Day in the Life of a Narcissist

Narcissism has a dark side and its impact on children, spouses, employees, other family members and entire communities can be devastating. There is no easy answer to dealing with a narcissist with uncontrolled rages, but they are inevitable and they rarely subside even with age.

Over the years, people with Narcissistic Personality Disorder have been leaving their imprint in the course of humanity. From their thoughts and behaviours, they have spurred several studies regarding the onset and the effects of narcissism on a person.

At the workplace, you might excessively demean your coworkers or attempt to gratify them in an attempt to get them to do whatever you want. You consider them a means to an end and do whatever it takes in order to have them satisfy whatever your given ends *are*. You will have an excessively hard time building strong relationships due to the fact that you simply don't or *aren't able* to act with the proper amount of empathy. People desire empathy in their interpersonal relationships and thrive off of having somebody who genuinely cares about them. You have to be able to do this in order to hold and maintain relationships and without this crucial ability, you're lacking an important characteristic.

When faced with tension either at home or at work, people with narcissistic personality disorder will frequently find themselves refusing to admit when they could be wrong in a given situation.

This leads to increased stress and tension. Mostly, however, they generally are unable to realise when they *are* wrong, or unwilling to admit that they are at risk of ruining their delusion.

As such, somebody who suffers from narcissistic personality disorder will be unable to have conducive arguments either at home or at the workplace. For this reason, people with this disorder may be unable to keep a job or stable relationships. When they do have stable relationships, they're categorised by abusive tendencies.

At home, people with narcissistic personality disorder will suffer from a generally poor home life of their own construction. Their inability to deal with conflict in a meaningful way and lack of ability to reflect upon themselves and their own behaviour will lead often to frustration on the partner's end.

Effects of Narcissistic Personality Disorder

When a person is suffering from this disorder, they can become prone to drug abuse and excessive intake of alcohol. They usually have a greater chance of being depressed and most often will have relationship problems. There are also issues of having difficulties at work or school. Worse still, they may have suicidal thoughts and exhibit suicidal behaviours.

Narcissistic Personality Disorder, which can affect every aspect of a person's wellbeing, which includes mental, physical and social wellbeing.

Generally, those that are living with Narcissistic Personality Disorder may appear as being too superior to get help or treatment.

Therefore, it is important to understand the extent at which this disorder can affect the life of your loved one. It will also help those that are suffering from the disorder improve their chances of deciding to get proper treatment their decision to get proper treatment for this mental health condition.

Most times, when a narcissist is a leader, they exhibit some selfish and exploitative leadership styles, but in the long run the flaws in their character will be revealed. With their grandiose attitudes, they find themselves devaluing their fellow employees and even disregarding corporate rules.

A person romantically involved with a narcissist will feel like they are always at fault for doing wrong. They get blamed for that wrong which causes that person to develop an inner conflict that can derail them mentally to the point of constant confusion and nervousness and guilt. Their partner will manipulate them and any situation in order to shift the blame and the narcissist does this with such expert prowess that the person who loves them is blinded by it - blinded because of it. It is an endless and mentally exhausting for the man or woman who is romantically involved with the narcissist, the person who loves that narcissist.

The effect narcissists have over us is exponential because they manipulate feelings, guilt-trip our emotions, and gaslight constantly. The need for demand and supply – the addiction to manipulating people and their emotions and or showing off – is such that the narcissist does not care about others but the euphoria of outdoing.

THE NARCISSIST IN POWER

When a narcissist is given access to unrestricted power through an organisation or institution, their empathy deficient attitudes can have a similar impact as in a family or social circle, but they often trickle down from the narcissistic source through other echelons of power, where they may be distorted, misunderstood, reframed, or disguised. Under these circumstances, it can be virtually impossible to trace problems back to their source, namely the narcissist in power, as they are in a perfect position to deflect, triangulate, dismiss complaints and re-assign blame to others. In this type of power structure, the narcissist has an endless source of narcissistic supply, being able to demand whatever type of attention they desire from inferiors at a moment's notice, without ever being expected to reciprocate or even express gratitude. Therefore, the narcissist can easily begin to view other members as replaceable; the institution becomes an extension of the narcissist's feelings of self-importance, and therefore the narcissist will stop at nothing to see it succeed, grow, and achieve its stated goals.

THE NARCISSISTIC TEACHER

It's especially heartbreaking to realise that most educational environments are set up to be ideal platforms for a narcissist to establish a regime. Academic institutions are competitive and hierarchical, and unlike many other walks of life, within them, the hierarchy is often fully transparent. Performances are rated or ranked by authority figures in public, and all students are made aware at some point that there are limited resources at the end of the road;

after graduation, some will achieve their goals, get accepted to another academic institution or land their dream job, while others – presumably those who underperform – will not.

The narcissistic teacher enters this environment already holding the keys to all their student's dreams. They may enjoy ruling the classroom through fear, enforcing strict (but unevenly applied) rules and accepting no less than whatever they define as "the best." Alternatively, a narcissistic teacher might enjoy admiration from their students – whether it's genuine or manufactured to receive better grades isn't important to the teacher, so long as it helps them to feel important and powerful. This type might spend most of their time in the classroom trying to charm the students, or perform their own magnificence for them, all the while forgetting to actually educate them on the relevant subject matter.

THE NARCISSISTIC BOSS

A narcissistic boss can make an employee's life a living hell. Under them, office cultures tend to be defined by constant nervousness and tension. Like the narcissistic teacher, they may use fear and intimidation tactics to secure their power over employees, or they may prefer to use charm and skill proficiency to win admiration from others. Either way, those who work underneath them are typically afraid to make any misstep, knowing that they won't be granted constructive criticism; instead, they'll either be verbally berated, humiliated, or simply fired – or, if charm is the narcissist's weapon of choice, their employee may simply be given the silent treatment and ignored for long periods without ever being told why.

Most narcissistic bosses will proudly claim that they ascended to the top through hard work or innate predisposition to the skill set required for the job. The sad truth, though, is that many are high achievers for no reason other than their inability to feel remorse. They routinely throw others under the bus, take credit for work that isn't theirs, and won't miss a beat in "getting over" the many personal and professional relationships they have to destroy in pursuit of their goals. Since they control worker's access to necessary funds, they rarely face direct criticism for these behaviours, and the "fact" that they deserve their position is hardly ever questioned, at least not publicly.

THE NARCISSISTIC PUBLIC FIGURE

If there's anything that can transform the average narcissist into a loaded weapon of a personality, it's fame. Celebrities and public figures are usually getting their egos boosted twenty-four hours a day, seven days a week, and are being paid a fortune to stand in the spotlight. They can actually build up a tolerance to this avalanche of positive attention, as an alcoholic build up a tolerance to alcohol, and once that happens, it's a slippery slope towards losing their entire grip on reality. They need to feel increasingly more and more powerful, but in the realm of fame, they come to realise they are competing mostly against other narcissists, and the competition is steep. It isn't exactly easy for one celebrity to get their fix of superiority by putting another down; since their lives are so public, such a gesture can backfire and end up diminishing their fan base. Therefore, their attempts to chase the initial rush that ascendance to fame provided can lead them towards eccentric, confusing, and desperate measures.

Narcissistic celebrity actors can sometimes lose sight of the fact they aren't capable of everything their characters are; for example, an actor playing a doctor might come to believe that they are actually qualified to practice medicine. In the same vein, narcissistic politicians get a lot of narcissistic supply from making promises, but actually enacting them often proves difficult and divisive to their voter bases; therefore, they may come to mentally equate promises with actual activity, feeling that once a promise passes over their lips, the deed is as good as done. It becomes difficult for all narcissists in public roles to discern the difference between lies and truths since lies must be told publicly on so many occasions.

Chapter 11: Use Your Observer Self to Increase Mindfulness

With Narcissistic Personality Disorder, the one thing you need to escape from is yourself. Often, people who have issues with narcissism are pretty hard on their selves as they would be with anyone else. Maintaining the idea that you are better, superior, or need attention makes you convinced that the idea is a fact and not just your opinion. The crux of the problem is people. Whether "people" means the person with the disorder or the people whom the narcissist deals with, people become the issue. The best way to escape is to be away from people and away from anything that will make you want to be critical of yourself. This means that a solitary hobby is the best route for someone with Narcissistic Personality Disorder. Meditation can also be hugely beneficial. Despite the route taken, something has to allow the person to have a mental escape from their selves.

Hobbies can be very entertaining, time consuming, and allow for inner focus. You have to find something that doesn't allow for heavy criticism or a need to feel competitive. The choice can be different for anyone. Maintaining a garden may be good for one person but may cause another to feel the need for the best plants and biggest production of fruits and such. The hobby cannot be something that can be paralleled with issues that are already a problem. A hobby can be reading a book, listening to or playing music, a collection of some sort, or small projects. As long as it is tailored in a way that does not feed into the narcissist's need for attention or competitive nature, something that takes up your free personal time can give you a break from the pressures of socialisation.

Meditation is one of the best things for anyone with problems that affect their social mentality. With meditation, whether you are alone or with a group, there is quiet and peace, and the focus is inward. Whether you are attractive, successful, more intelligent, or whatever, in meditation these things no longer matter. They also do not have any effect on the process of meditation. With a clear mind and a focus on something pleasant, distant, or deep within, the challenges and difficulties with other people is washed away. Meditation can be done in many settings, at any time, can last for any amount of time, and is fairly easy to do. With the implementation of something like meditation in your life, you will have a better understanding of yourself through inner reflection and thus a better understanding of people's core and not the superficial things we base each other off of.

Mindfulness allows you to have thoughts that are in the present, and it creates a calming feeling that helps with both stress and anxiety.

Some people might find mindfulness difficult to practice, especially those with anxious, hyperactive minds. When faced with an anxiety-inducing situation, it can be easy to forget to take time to be calm and remain in the moment. Whether you're hoping to go to a party or contemplating trying a new dance class at the community centre, your anxious thoughts will often try to convince you not to take a chance. In that moment, try to simply observe these unhelpful thoughts and let them pass.

Meditation can be a very helpful tool throughout this process. Begin by sitting comfortably in a space that is quiet and free of distraction. Practice breathing slowly and taking deep breaths each time you breathe in. Focus on your body in space and feel each part of your body as you breathe. There are several guided meditations available online for you to peruse if you so desire, or you may choose to come up with your own little mantra. Whatever you decide to do, try to make some time each and every day to focus in on your affirmation. Repeat the words to yourself slowly, over and over. Tell yourself that you love yourself, that you forgive yourself, that you are enough, that you are loved, that you are strong. Simply saying these words to yourself will begin to break the toxic habit and thought cycles that once plagued your mind and triggered anxiety. Eventually, you will come to a place where those negative feelings are no longer connected to the obsessive thoughts that intruded on your mind. As you practice replacing these bad thoughts with positive ones, it will become habitual and begin to feel more natural. Meditation can be kind of strange for first-time practitioners, but I encourage you to give it a try if you are struggling to move past those negative obsessive thought cycles.

It's okay to feel challenged by the practice of mindfulness. When you feel challenged, it means you're trying something new that's triggering your growth. When practicing mindfulness while also dealing with social anxiety, remember to be compassionate with yourself during the process. It's easy to feel frustrated when you can't stay present and observe what's going on in your mind or body without getting caught up in it. When you have a hard time being present in the moment, it's easy to say to oneself, *I can't do this*. Remind yourself that it takes time and practice. Nobody perfects mindfulness on the first try—or the second.

And when you practice mindfulness, you tune your thoughts into what you are sensing in the present moment as opposed to imagining the future or rehashing the past.

Mindfulness can help reverse the tunnel vision that tends to develop in our everyday life, particularly when you are tired, stressed out or busy. It can be easy to stop paying attention to the world around you. It is also easy to lose touch with the way your body is feeling and to find yourself living in your head: entangled in your own thoughts without stopping to realise how these thoughts are influencing your behaviour and emotions.

Mindfulness can help you to reconnect with your body and the sensations it experiences. This means waking up to the tastes, smells, sounds and sights of the present moment. This could be as simple as the smell of that rosemary as you go to work.

Another significant part of mindfulness is the awareness of your thoughts and feelings as they occur from moment to moment.

This kind of awareness does not start by trying to fix or change anything; it is about allowing yourself to clearly see the present moment without passing judgment. Once you do this, it can positively change the way you see yourself and your life.

So why should you be mindful in the first place? Why is it necessary to practice mindfulness?

Mindfulness is a practice of accessing your true essence. You live in the moment, thinking about only that moment, instead of what is worrying, stressful, or fearful. You place your mind in the reality of your surroundings, assessing if there are any current dangers, to help your mind realise there is nothing to be fearful about at the moment. You use the power of intention and curiosity to live a life without judgment. Only you can stop the thoughts you feel or think others have about you. Focus on observations rather than conjecture. It is easy to put thoughts and words into other's minds when you feel these things about yourself.

Only you can stop yourself from assigning emotions that are not reality, whether it is social anxiety, generalised anxiety, or another type of anxiety disorder. Anxiety disorders do not include paranoia or delusions unless you have more than one mental illness. Yes, fear is irrational when there is no context for the emotion, but you can overcome it by facing the reality that danger is not present.

Chapter 12: Difference between Healthy Narcissism and extreme Narcissism

Unhealthy Narcissism vs. Healthy Narcissism

There is a difference here. Some people might view a highly confident person as somewhat narcissistic. However, the easiest way to distinguish between the two is to look at their behaviour and personality as a whole. One of the greatest elements that allow you to tell the difference is to see if the person is humble. A narcissist is unable to be humble, but someone who is simply highly confident can exhibit strong self-esteem, but still be humble.

When someone is considered to have healthy narcissism, it means that they can get through difficult times by experiencing joy in themselves. This is associated with self-worth and self-esteem. Healthy narcissism is often fleeting. This means that a person likely does not feel amazing and inflated at all times based on who they are. This is because it does not have the same preoccupation that is present with unhealthy narcissism. However, this essentially kicks in when they do some self-reflection, look for the silver lining during a hard time or when they accomplish something, such as graduating from college or completing a big project at work.

Healthy narcissism is actually a good thing. It can be very helpful for those needing to get through a setback or a difficult time. For example, if a person is working a lot and starting to get burned out, the pleasure they get from completing a big project can give them what they need to power through and actually avoid complete burnout.

Healthy narcissism also feeds into healthy self-love. It allows people to be humble, but to also be proud of what they have accomplished. They also respect limits and know when to shine and when to allow others to have the spotlight. They know that with this balance, they will get praise when it is warranted, but it never causes negative feelings when another person is in the spotlight. In fact, they will ensure that they give the person in the spotlight praise. It is essentially an act of equal give and take.

It is important to stay mindful of the fact that narcissism is not inherently evil. It exists for the sake of self-preservation, and therefore all of us should forgive ourselves for possessing some occasional narcissistic attitudes and impulses. What's important is to find a healthy balance between narcissism and empathy, which lie at opposite ends of a scale. A person who is hyper-empathetic or hyper-sensitive typically needs more narcissism than they naturally possess, and is liable to leave themselves vulnerable to harm without it; by contrast, a person who falls on the far end of the narcissistic spectrum will undoubtedly exhibit a deficiency of empathetic sensitivity.

We all need some empathy to function within society, but we also need to be somewhat selfish and detached from our empathetic perceptions from time to time. As a culture, we tend to deify the idea of a completely selfless individual, but in real-world experience, people who are entirely selfless can be grating, miserable, and difficult to deal with. They also teach others to view and treat them as inferior when they consistently put their own needs last. They empathise with everyone and thus can become drowned in emotional experiences. By contrast, we vilify the idea of a completely self-centred individual to the point of envisioning them as a demon or monster, with no soul and no emotional substance. In reality, though, a narcissist can be awfully charming and fun to be around – for short periods of time, at least. They train others to see them as superior by consistently putting their own needs first. And while their thought patterns are distorted in such a way as to stifle empathetic practice, narcissists experience the same range of emotions as most other people. Their emotions simply prompt them to behave differently. Under the surface, they are no different than anyone else.

When you find a healthy medium between these two attitudes, you are able to maintain healthy, reciprocal, and fairly easy relationships, because you are able to compromise reasonably. This ability to fluctuate between our empathetic and narcissistic impulses is what allows us to give to charitable causes when we have money to spare, but skip the donations when our personal funds are low so that we can still afford to feed ourselves. It allows us to ignore another person in need if we are buried under the weight of our own struggles, but reach out to them when we are better able to offer support. It also allows us to be ambitious and try new things that we haven't yet trained ourselves for, silencing the voice of self-doubt inside our heads. It allows us to maintain close, intimate relationships with others without growing entirely codependent or reliant upon them. It allows us to make healthy choices for ourselves, even in the face of resistance, opposition, or peer pressure.

The narcissist feels entitled to put their own needs ahead of everyone else's, even when the circumstances should prompt them to do just the opposite. They also have trouble putting themselves in the shoes of those around them, so they struggle to comprehend why their requests might be seen as unreasonable, or why their expectations might be difficult for others to meet. They don't notice or care when they cause other people inconvenience; meanwhile, a hyper-empath will care too much about inconveniencing others and feel the impulse to accommodate by minimising their own needs.

You may have exhibited some behaviours in your life that you now look back on as self-centred, showy, or lacking in empathy; you may even acknowledge some current desires or feelings that are self-centred. For the most part, this is normal, and not always an indication of a looming diagnosis. It is notably common for adolescents to display especially narcissistic attitudes, but generally speaking, this is a phase that people gradually grow out of as they learn to manage the ego in concert with their newly awakened sexual impulses. As adults, many of us have a tendency to lean a little further into our narcissistic sides when recovering from a rejection or a bruised ego, which is also perfectly acceptable and not necessarily an indication of an underlying personality disorder. Narcissism as a trait can be used to achieve positive ends, but as a creed, it erases empathy and causes deep emotional turmoil. If you are curious as to where you land on this spectrum, there are a number of free self-assessment tests available online to measure your empathy quotient – but bear in mind, this is not an exact science, nor are results set in stone. If you wish to display more or less empathy in your life, don't rely exclusively on tests to steer you towards the best course of action. Look to the world around you like your mirror; ask questions of your friends and peers with a willingness to make yourself vulnerable (but not submissive); experiment with different behaviours and methods of processing emotion. You may take some missteps, but that is perfectly fine because your mistakes do not define you.

Now that we have defined the difference between narcissism as a personality trait and narcissism as a personality disorder, henceforth, all references to narcissism or narcissists in this book will refer to the far end of the spectrum, implying a severe lack of empathy and consistently warped thought processes.

WHY IS HEALTHY NARCISSISM IMPORTANT?

If you are capable of experiencing and retaining the feeling of ecstatic euphoria in yourself, then you will have the necessary strength to overcome any difficulties you face in life. For instance, if you are capable of deriving happiness from accomplishing a difficult task at work, then it will give you the confidence and the resilience required to work through any frustrating times. Not just that, it also reduces the chances of potential burnout. Likewise, if you can take joy in your beauty and your ability to have a positive effect on others, it will give you the willpower to keep going even in the face of heartbreak or disappointments.

Some individuals can neither develop nor hold onto this sense of positive self-love. A lot of reasons can cause this—a narcissistic parent might demand all of the child's attention and praise, thereby leaving little room for the child to celebrate herself.

Some kids never cultivate positive narcissism because they are scared that others will envy them. When a child forms a mental association that they will be treated with hostility if they do well, then the child will try to hide or even lessen his excellence. Not just that, the child might start hiding it even from himself.

Do you feel wrong or guilty when you try to take pride in your good qualities? Do you think that others will be envious of you if you excel or that others might think you are conceited if you take pride in yourself? If you think this, then it is essential that you start developing some healthy narcissism. Healthy narcissism is the ability to be grateful for all the good that you have in life. It is about being grateful for all your talents and the ability to appreciate the same without becoming egotistical.

Here are all the elements of healthy narcissism:

You must not worry too much about the opinions others have about you. A true narcissist might make it seem like he doesn't care about what others think, but the truth is that he deeply cares about what others think of him. You might have heard that in your 20s you tend to worry about what others think of you, in your 40s you will not be bothered with what others think of you, and in your 60s you will finally realise that no one really thinks about you. Well, it seems like narcissists don't grow out of their 20s. The ideal thing to do is to not care about what everyone thinks of you and instead care only about what your loved ones think about you. Care here doesn't refer to your success or the praise you receive, it refers to whether they feel like you respect them, feel safe enough with you to be their true selves and sincerely wish for your wellbeing.

You must not take things personally. A narcissist will take everything personally because, in his mind, he is the centre of the universe. The slightest whiff of criticism will be taken as a personal assault, and it will make him paranoid. The healthy way to go about interacting with others is to treat others as your equals and to work on empathy. For instance, if your coworker was rude to you about something, don't jump to the conclusion that it was a personal attack. Instead, talk to your coworker about it; maybe he is dealing with some problem that put them in a bad mood.

Remember that it's okay to focus on you. Self-care and self-love are important for your wellbeing. As long as you don't cross over into the egotistical territory, it is all good.

A narcissist will never take responsibility for his actions and will think of ways in which the blame can be transferred onto others or the circumstances. Please don't do this. While developing healthy narcissism, you must learn to accept responsibility for your actions. No one forced you to act as you did, and you are the only one who can control your actions. It will do you good to remember this simple fact.

Different Types of Narcissist

There are many different kinds of narcissist out there, while reading these descriptions, stay mindful of the fact that these types are not fixed; a narcissist can evolve from one type into another, or even embody a unique blend of two or more types.

The grandiose or exhibitionist narcissist is the kind of person that we typically think of when we imagine a narcissist cliché. Generally speaking, they are extremely vain, condescending and arrogant, bold and charismatic, bombastic, and unashamed of their quest to acquire limitless power and prestige.

They are often so audacious in their narcissistic statements and behaviours that some will presume they are being sarcastic or comedic when they are in fact being quite genuine. People may laugh it off when this person mocks those that they consider beneath them, or launches into a monologue of self-praise, thinking that this is a show put on for the sake of entertaining others, ironically failing to see that this is the narcissist's honest expression of personal opinion. Unfortunately, reactions of laughter or silent acceptance can serve to reinforce the narcissist's inflated sense of self-importance, as they interpret these as signs of agreement or approval.

Grandiose narcissists also tend to have a childlike lack of self-awareness, choosing behaviours that virtually scream, "Look at me! Look at me!" They are usually comfortable speaking highly of themselves while belittling others with such brazen confidence that one might wonder if they have never been taught that such behaviour is considered rude.

This narcissistic type is likely to have the least shame in expressing their egocentric attitudes; this may be due to their genuine belief that they are obviously and strikingly better than everyone around them, and the accompanying assumption that this flamboyant pea-cocking is what others expect of them. For example, if a member of a foreign country's royal family met you but refused to shake your hand or make eye contact, you might accept their display of arrogance, in light of their title. A grandiose narcissist might struggle to understand why you wouldn't extend the same courtesy and respect to them. Though you may see yourself as more or less their equal, they believe themselves to be superior to you and everyone else, so their haughtiness and vanity are justified in their minds.

THE CLOSET NARCISSIST

The closet narcissist is also called a "covert" narcissist. They have the same competitive, defensive, and shame avoidant mindset as any other narcissist type, but they express it in a stealthy way, flying under the radar. While a grandiose narcissist can be loud and showy, using bravado to mask their insecurities, the closet narcissist's preferred tactic is silence. This isn't a submissive or reticent silence, it is pointed and deliberate. While keeping their lips sealed, they are able to assert their status and superiority by judging others and ever refusing to make themselves vulnerable to similar judgment.

While the grandiose narcissist never misses a chance to hog the spotlight, the closet narcissist feels conflicted about their thirst for attention. They may have been raised in a household with another grandiose narcissist who would not tolerate competition; alternatively, they might have been raised to see any explicit bid for attention as tacky or undignified and therefore learned to become an expert at seeking attention in stealthy, underhanded ways. They commonly use snobbery to belittle others, looking down their noses at them rather than explicitly insulting them with words.

Self-image is often deeply important to them, but the closet narcissist would be reluctant to talk about this or let others see how much work goes into manufacturing the face, body, and dress they present to the exterior world. For example, a closet narcissist could become obsessed with exercise, perfecting their body shape through hours and hours of work at the gym each week – but when offered a compliment on their sculpted figure, they would not want to admit that it took effort on their part, preferring instead to pretend that the shape is natural and easy for them to carry. Or, they might admit to the hard work but claim they were motivated by health or happiness, rather than a desperate need to be admired.

In short, a closet narcissist is a master of disguise, using feigned humility, shyness or a charitable demeanour to mask the self-centred motivations behind all of their actions. They may not be likely to brag about their achievements, financial successes, or romantic conquests, and they might not draw attention to themselves through physical grooming or dynamic, showy behaviours; instead, this type is more likely to seek attention from others in the form of sympathy or pity. Rather than drawing attention to their own good looks, skills, or talents, they might spend conversations belittling or invalidating the achievements and appearances of other people, with the silent implication of personal superiority. At a dinner party, the grandiose narcissist might feel no shame in claiming the seat at the head of the table in someone else's home, and helping themselves to the first and largest serving of food; the closet narcissist wouldn't take either of these actions, but instead might become offended and resentful of the fact that these courtesies weren't offered to them automatically.

Alternatively, the closet narcissist might define their self-worth and feel special based on their proximity to something unique, desirable, and unattainable – or their relationship with a person who embodies the same qualities. For example, a closet narcissist may not be particularly boastful or ostentatious about it, but choose to dress in elite designer brands from head to toe, hoping that only other special people of a similar degree of importance might recognise them as a member of the same club. Or, they might find their source of superiority by befriending celebrities or powerful politicians. Covert narcissists tend to make excellent assistants to high-powered bosses, talent managers, and behind-the-scenes orchestrators; just beyond the reach of the spotlight, they can stand beside the star and pull all the strings from a comfortable, well-shielded position.

They struggle to maintain personal relationships or start them since they aren't as confident, charismatic, or overtly charming as their grandiose counterparts. When they do build any type of close relationship, though, they often develop a two-faced demeanour, presenting one personality to the outside world and exhibiting just the opposite when alone with a "loved" one.

Like the grandiose narcissist, the closet narcissist can develop their personality disorder as a response to narcissistic abuse in childhood. While they possess a deep understanding of the grandiose and malignant narcissists' mindsets and could offer tremendous insight to the recovery community, they choose the path of defensiveness over empathy, embracing the idea that "if you can't beat them, you might as well join them." Since they spend so much time within their heads, a closet narcissist may be the most likely of the three to eventually seek treatment, healing, and change, but they will only be able to do so if they are pushed to admit their vulnerability. Otherwise, their deeply self-conscious mindset becomes a self-reinforcing prison that can pull them further and further away from the connection to reality over time.

THE MALIGNANT NARCISSIST

Malignant or toxic narcissists are rarer than both the grandiose or covert types, which is lucky for the rest of us. If you've ever known a true malignant narcissist, you understand what a volatile and destructive force this personality disorder can be. People who earn this title typically suffer from a combination of narcissistic personality disorder along with one or more others, such as antisocial personality disorder, manic or compulsive behavioural issues, paranoia, or sadistic inclinations. They are often the easiest narcissists to recognise, as they are usually unable to achieve the same degrees of success that grandiose or covert narcissists can grasp.

Without real evidence of their superiority, in the form of money, status, power, educational degrees, or social support, it can be overwhelmingly obvious to others that the malignant narcissist has an unrealistic opinion of their own importance. It is not obvious to the malignant narcissist, though.

Malignant narcissists tend to see the world through a lens of dichotomies, the most important of which is "me versus everyone and everything else." They have trouble understanding grey areas or multifaceted concepts, preferring to define everything as either good or bad, right or wrong, love or hate, yes or no, now or never. They also have an impulse to turn everything into a competition, applying the logic of scarcity to circumstances where it isn't necessary; for example, at a pizza party with more food and more seating than is needed to accommodate everyone's needs, the malignant narcissist might get bent out of shape over who takes the largest slice of any particular pie, or who claims the seat that they consider most optimal, even though there's more than enough to go around.

They often create mountains out of molehills and spin up trouble out of thin air. They see chaos as the stage upon which they perform best, providing ample opportunity for them to manipulate others and secure further power for themselves. Regardless of any social or financial stability they secure for themselves as adults, they are mentally stuck in survival mode; this means that when they perceive another person as a threat, they can quickly and easily leap to a disproportionate self-defensive gesture.

While both the grandiose and covert narcissist aim to maintain a certain level of respectability in regards to their reputation and therefore keep their unsavoury attitudes reigned in at some degree, the malignant narcissist appears to be unmoved by the disapproval of others, and uninhibited in their expressions of negativity and egocentricity. For example, when on the receiving end of a public slight, all three types of narcissist would feel the impulse to retaliate; however, the grandiose narcissist might be compelled to consider their audience and exact vengeance in the form of a witty comeback, or to wait until a more private moment to express their rage; the covert narcissist would be similarly driven to save face in public, and would perhaps be most likely to seek revenge by spreading rumours, or finding an anonymous way to get back at their foe. By contrast, the malignant narcissist would be most likely to react immediately and escalate the conflict through yelling, name calling, and perhaps even physical violence.

The malignant narcissist is the most dangerous of the three types. At times, their behaviour can be indistinguishable from that of the criminally psychopathic. They see no problem with causing pain for others as a means to an end; in some cases, they may even derive pleasure from causing emotional or physical harm to their victims, enjoying the rush of sadistic power it provides for them.

The 3 Subtypes of Narcissistic Personality Disorder

GRANDIOSE

With this specific group, there is a pressured attitude towards others. They feel they are owed respect or subservience based on the delusion that they are smarter, stronger, or in some other way, better than everyone else. Bullies often belong to this subtype. A bully will pick on, torture, harass, and further aggravate people simply because they are operating under the idea that they are significantly more superior and thus, not someone who has to lower themselves to anyone else, regardless of who they really are. This can be almost a coping mechanism for these people. If you are unable to deal with the fact that you are bigger, poorer, uglier, etc., than everyone else, there can be situations where that pent up anger is taken out on others of the same standing. It can almost seem like a vicarious self-punishment. By making others cower to them, grandiose personality types feel better about themselves and their own situation. This, in turn, convinces them that what they tell themselves about how great they are is true. The reaction of people around them due to their persona will confirm their own beliefs and allow the cycle to continue. Usually, if you have a grandiose personality subtype of narcissism, it is a cover for a deeper issue with self-esteem and image. They use brutality and aggression to make themselves feel better and to back up their false image. Having this image questioned or shattered can be quite devastating to them, and can sometimes lead to a violent outburst. With narcissism in general, it is hard to make any comments against what they say or believe. Trying to tell a grandiose personality subtype that they are not as big or as smart or as strong or whatever they may think is equivalent to completely disrespecting them. It's a huge offence against them and their personality and clashes with how they see themselves. This, in turn, makes them defensive and can cause a greater deal of arrogance and hostility. The balance is not there to keep them from tilting too far. There is a very fine line between their arrogance and their own self-loathing. It does not take much to blur the line and cause them to take out this self-loathing on the person who has insulted them in any way.

VULNERABLE

Vulnerable, or fragile, subtypes of Narcissistic Personality Disorder can be difficult to pinpoint. These people do not seem like they have narcissistic issues, but more like they are just attention-seeking.

Hypochondriacs, people with Munchausen and Munchausen by Proxy Syndrome are clearly in this category. Hypochondriacs believe there is something wrong with them when there is not. They may believe they have a rare illness or a plethora of illnesses and will hound medical professionals with these conditions. They often take a multitude of medications and supplements to treat their perceived conditions. Most actually do believe they are suffering from what they claim to have. Munchausen syndrome is when a patient creates or severely enhances a medical issue. Munchausen by Proxy Syndrome is when someone purposefully makes someone else, often a child, ill or sicker than they actually are, simply to gain attention and sympathy from others. These people feel they deserve special treatment due to hardships, either real or perceived, in their life. This subtype usually has the deepest set of background disorders. Depression, anxiety, body dysmorphic syndrome, underlying actual health issues, self-image and esteem issues, and sometimes even a history of abuse or neglect. If you have a vulnerable personality type, you feed on the pity and attention of others. They seek empathy by utilising people's concern for them to heighten their need for attention. By creating or exaggerating illnesses, personal wrongs, abuse, neglect and other issues, they are able to represent themselves as victims. Lying can be a major issue with this personality subtype as it creates the basis for their story.

EXHIBITIONISTIC

Like the grandiose, they believe they are better than everyone else in one form or fashion. Unlike grandiose subtypes however, exhibitionistic often actually have the qualities to back up their beliefs. This is the arrogance you see in someone that is very rich, attractive, and/or successful. Such arrogance is often due to having wealth, a high position in their job, an above average intelligence, and/or very attractive physical attributes. When you have an exhibitionistic behaviour, you will have very little to dissuade you from your belief of superiority. In order for a narcissist to understand the level of ordinary people, they need a humbling factor. People with grandiose personalities lack the humbling factor because their beneficial situation goes a long way to confirm and back up their beliefs. It is easy to feel a sense of intimidation from these people, as they will have an "air of superiority" (as they say) about them. The arrogance that goes with the idea can often be their downfall too. Someone highly successful can be brought down by greed or the inability to manage the fruits of that success. For them, being anything less than great is out of the question. Having their greatness reduced is a significant blow to the psyche. These people live by their successful persona and depend on it for the very basis of their behaviour and personality.

The most difficult aspect to this personality type is that they do have the life or lifestyle to back up their expectations and declarations about themselves. Furthermore, there is often a family tradition of such behaviour. If the person is successful and wealthy, they probably come from a successful and wealthy family that has the same pomposity about themselves. As it is so deeply ingrained, it is even harder to pinpoint, much less deal with. These subtypes will very rarely ever be convinced they have a problem; much less will they ever try to change how they feel and act. In movies, the rich man falls for a poor woman and after seeing how she lives, he begins to analyse his own life and live a less arrogant and narcissistic lifestyle. This rarely happens in real life though. First of all, a person who sees themselves as being of high standing is not going to subject themselves to something they see as below their station. Secondly, even if it did happen, it is more likely that the less well-off party will succumb to a more arrogant state of mind rather than pull the other person down to their level. Wealth and success is usually something that severely changes a person, no matter how much people would like to think otherwise. The company they begin keeping, the ability to have what they want when they want it, and how people treat them, can easily inadvertently lead to a narcissistic state of mind. Thus, in this scenario, the high-functioning narcissist has now created a grandiose narcissist.

Chapter 13: First Steps of Recovery from Narcissistic abuse

To kick start your recovery process, it is first necessary to understand what makes the narcissist tick. It's easier to recover from the abuse when you know what and who you're dealing with. By "what", I mean the methods used by the narcissist to manipulate you, the motivation behind the narc's actions and the resulting changes in how you see yourself. By "who", I mean the narcissist as a person. A narcissistic parent will act and react differently than a narcissistic "friend" or lover. You know what narcissism is and you know how to deal with it. The next step is making sure that you have what is needed to truly heal from the experience. This is a process, and no one expects you to just forget the issue never happened. Working on yourself and putting yourself first is what will allow you to get over the negative consequences of your experience.

Life would be much simpler if everything could be controlled, but this is not possible. When you find something that you have no control over, recognise it and let it go. For example, not every person will like you, and there are times when a loved one may get mad at you for something that is not your fault. Do not press the issue. Let it go, and everything will eventually work itself out in the end.

There are simpler things that you can start doing on a regular basis to start pushing out negative emotions and helping to enhance your overall well-being. You do not have to do every single one on a daily basis but consider them and incorporate them into your day when it is appropriate. These include:

- Get proactive and do not allow the negative to just settle into your life
- When life gets tough, cry it out because this can aid in reducing stress
- Scream as loud as you can for a few seconds as this naturally counteracts negative emotions
- Get some sleep since it is easier to tackle stress and negative emotions when you are not exhausted
- Try to be positive and no matter what happens, force yourself to find the silver lining in the situation
- Take a few minutes to laugh every day since when you are laughing, negative emotions cannot be present
- Find someone you trust who care about you and talk to them when you need to get help with a problem
- Consider an alternate perspective to see if it might allow you to better solve a problem
- Forgive yourself for setbacks as long as you recognise them and do not allow them to completely throw you off track
- Own your feelings and when negative emotions occur, recognise them, consider why you are experiencing them and then detach from it
- Write about the day or experience you just had before going to bed each night because this allows you to leave the negative in the past so you can start fresh the next day

Make a learning opportunity out of every mistake. Every person fails and makes mistakes. This is part of life. However, do not dwell on these and the negative consequences that might come with them. Spend an hour being upset because it is important to experience your emotions. However, after an hour, go into action mode and consider why the mistake or failure occurred. You will always be able to find at least one lesson. This lesson reduces the risk of mistakes and failure in the future.

Know that perfection is simply not possible. What's important is that you're putting in the effort and working to learn and get better. No person is born automatically being great at everything. Life is all about learning and working on developing the skills needed to achieve your goals.

Remember that every person has their own strengths. Imagine a world where every person is just good at everything. There would be no healthy competition, no learning, and no balance. Know your strengths and respect the strengths of others.

Know what you cannot change. For example, if you are short, you are short. You cannot change this. Once you accept what cannot be changed, you can start putting your focus on the areas of your life that can be improved.

Don't be afraid to try. You never know what you are good at until you test your limits. Have you always wanted to play soccer, but were afraid you were not good enough? Get a game going with friends or join a local team. You may be great, or you may not. Either way, you tried it, and every new thing you try expands your horizons.

Give yourself credit when you deserve it. When you do something great, be proud of yourself. It is easy to put more focus on flaws because this is just what humans do. However, when you switch your focus to the good stuff, your self-esteem will get a big boost.

QUESTIONING YOURSELF

If you think you have Narcissistic Personality Disorder, you do have options. Although it can be difficult, you have the opportunity and the ability to take charge of your life and deal effectively this pervasive disorder. There are thing that you can do to help yourself and the people around you. By engaging in these activities and taking responsibility for yourself, you can improve your life.

First, you need to understand and accept that you have a problem with the way you deal with the world. Once you admit that you have a narcissistic personality, you can move forward and try to act in more socially acceptable ways. It is important that you know exactly who you are and how you behave.

In order to do this, you should sit down make a list of the behaviours that you engage in that are maladaptive, destructive, or self-defeating. Admit what behaviours are causing the most problems in your life. Then, make another list of the behaviours you engage in that are helpful and constructive, or productive. You should try to engage in more of the behaviours on the second list and try to avoid the behaviours on the first list.

When the attention is diverted elsewhere, this can make the narcissist feel very alone. This is true even if they are surrounded by multiple people. They put a lot of emphasis on attention and adoration, so anytime they aren't flooded with it, they can feel unwanted and isolated. So, you've gotten away from the toxic influence and started to work on yourself and your own life. You're finally at a point where you're comfortable focusing on your mental health. What are the steps that you can take in order to clean up the wreckage of the physical and emotional abuse of a relationship with a narcissist?

Admitting to yourself that you're ready to assert the things that have gone wrong for you is a big step, first off, and I'd really like to commend you for getting this far. It's not easy to get to this point, and a lesser person would start to falter right around now. However, you are not small. If you were, you never would have left in the first place.

The first thing that I can really recommend you do in this position is to start doing whatever you can in order to reach out to professionals. Specifically, it'd be wise if you looked into finding a counsellor or a therapist, preferably a therapist. A therapist is the perfect person for you to visit because they'll give you an impartial party with whom you can look back at the stuff that happened or look at the way it affects your personality now - as well as a person who can give you general life advice as things move forward - and they'll look critically at the psychology of what you're doing and why which gives you an opportunity to apply your focus more and more on what has gone wrong for you internally and how you can fix it.

Therapists are expensive, unfortunately. Counsellors are generally available in subsidised locations like women's shelters who aren't quite as knowledgeable or experienced about the raw psychology as therapists are but who are nevertheless trained to help you deal with abuse specifically. If your healthcare insurance won't cover a therapist, then you can most likely make ends meet for a counsellor. With that said, most therapists will charge $50 to $150 an hour, and if you can spare that expense even paying out of pocket, it's worth it to get the expertise that a therapist has to offer.

It's important to also note that you won't always find the right professional right off the bat. A good therapist or counsellor match is a person who you feel comfortable with and whose specific methodology in terms of psychology and therapy fits what you personally mesh well with. Everybody has a different style of psychology and therapy and while there are general best practices—for example, the general path for cognitive behavioural therapy is usually the same—the general setup and layout of a given therapist's sessions will be highly dependent upon themselves as a therapist. You aren't even going to like the way different therapists may decorate their rooms compared to another therapist. There are a million little variables that go into comfort. Don't get discouraged if your first one or two visits with different therapists aren't terribly conducive.

After you've set up some kind of routine with a therapist or counsellor, it's time that you start forging new friendships. Hopefully, if you're working, then you've already got some coworkers that you can start hanging out with. Get to know the people around you and get closer to them. There may be some good in people that you never saw before. It's harder now than ever to open up to somebody and really let them see who *you* are, and indeed, you shouldn't sacrifice your vulnerability so easily - after an abusive relationship, you may be especially prone to letting people make you feel like you're worth less than you really are - but you should allow yourself to be vulnerable with somebody if they're willing to be vulnerable with you and if they aren't showing any obvious red flags that indicate malicious intent.

GETTING RETRIBUTION AND REWARDING YOURSELF

Next, you need to be willing to punish yourself when you engage in the behaviours on the first list. What can you do to discourage yourself to engage in these behaviours? Write these things down, and, when you find yourself engaging in the negative behaviours, you have to be willing to do them.

On the other side, make a list of positive rewards or prizes for engaging in the adaptive behaviours. When you act in an acceptable and appropriate manner, give yourself a reward from your second list. Rewards and negative reinforcement help teach people what is and is not acceptable. If you are willing to change your behaviour, you can do so by being aware of your behavioural responses and responding to them accordingly.

The key is to be consistent in administering the negative reinforcers and the positive rewards when you engage in certain behaviours. You need to do it all the time. You must be willing to look at your behaviours objectively to administer such punishments and rewards. If you are able to do so, you can decrease the frequency of your problem and your behaviours and encourage yourself to engage in the positive behaviours. These things can be done on your own or under the supervision of a therapist. Any loved one in your life may also be willing to help you change your behaviours in this way. A therapist can be very helpful in learning to identify which behaviours are problematic and which are not, and coming up with positive and negative reinforcers for you.

These can be difficult steps to follow. However, once you are willing to admit that you have a problem and are willing to monitor your behaviours, you can make major changes in your life. You will get along better with others and your life should get easier. But you cannot let your guard down. Unfortunately, NPD is pervasive and doesn't have a cure. But, with diligence, you can control your behaviours and lead a much better life.

In conjunction with therapy and possibly medication to treat associated psychiatric symptoms, your NPD can be controlled. For example, if you have anxiety associated with your illness, you can take anti-anxiety meds to help deal with this. Take heart that you have your own future in your hands. You can make the decision to take positive steps to live a better life.

ADMIT THE PROBLEM

Admission of a problem is the most difficult thing anyone has to face. Realising that there is a problem, putting a name to it, and then deciding to do something about it is a pretty significant step for anyone facing a disorder in which they rarely, if ever, deviate from their beliefs. With Narcissistic Personality Disorder, the overall issue is the perceived superiority. Being that this normally dismisses any evidence contrary to how the person feels and believes, someone else trying to point out that it is a problem will often be stopped from trying to have the argument with the person. If you have Narcissistic Personality Disorder, the best approach is for you to come to your own conclusions about why you have such a negative perspective on the people around you. Realising that it is not usual for someone to consistently see themselves as being better than everyone is a hard fact to face. At that point, you have to progress from the realisation of the disorder to deciding to better yourself by learning about it and learning how to overcome the disorder.

SEPARATION & INVITATION

You identify with a certain way of being and living. You are aware of some of your capabilities, talents and dreams and you have a certain outlook on life. At the beginning you're *Living in Denial*. You're in the illusion, fantasy, idea of what your life could be but you're largely unaware of the reality that you're actually living in. On the daily you're stuffing away your feelings to get by. You're minimising and invalidating yourself, and possibly desperately seeking validation from others but worse yet there may not even be many others to get validation from.

You're not really fulfilled or happy and maybe you are kind of want to fix that, but at the same time you don't want to because it seems like such a drag to do anything about it. In this early stage there's a sense of complacency. If you're somewhat honest with yourself in this phase, perhaps you'll notice that you have an unresolved desire in your heart and an unexpressed song in your soul. At this point you've still got a limited self-awareness of your wound and that's exactly what's blocking you.

At first everything is seemingly "fine." Yet underneath the surface, some part of you senses that you're pretending everything is okay. You're probably living in a state of ignorance, denial, and rationalisations, though you're largely unaware of that yet. You have a rationalisation for everything that you're allowing in your life and you're comfortable with that because it feels normal.

FIND THE SOURCE

Usually, finding a solid source of the affliction is the best way to decide how to deal with the problem. A history of being coddled, spoiled, overprotected, or in some way made to think you are better for one reason or another is a starting point. From this knowledge, you are able to surmise how you formed the opinions that now form your current ideas on yourself and others. You cannot change how you were raised or the genetics that give you the feelings you have about yourself and people, but you can use the base experience to reevaluate how you are and how feel now. The saying is that you must pull it out by the roots. This is true with many behaviour disorders. Finding the source, figuring out how such sources affected you, and then deciding how you can use the initial situation to change your current one will go a long way in helping you overcome your disorders.

LEARN TO RELATE

If you have Narcissistic Personality Disorder, you usually have a hard time relating to others. Your inability to empathise makes it hard for you to understand exactly why others feel the way they do. Putting yourself in the shoes of the people around you can be very challenging. The only way to really relate, then, is for you to focus on the insecurities that cause you to build the wall. For instance, knowing that your body build makes you feel insecure can help you understand why someone else does not like being seen as unattractive or less attractive. If you are already facing this and cover it up by telling yourself and others how good you look, then you can understand why someone would be offended by your behaviour. With this you can then focus on treating people more how you wish to be treated. The old adage isn't far from the truth and states just as much: if you want respect, then you must give your respect to others.

KEEP YOURSELF IN CHECK

After you've taken steps to try to change your outlook in life, yourself, and other people, you must maintain that outlook. It is very easy to slip back into old habits, and criticising others with the intent to feel better than them can be very simple to do. Once you have faced your situation, began understanding how you approach yourself and everyone else, you then have the tools to combat the thoughts that you deal with. This goes back to the idea of treating others the way you want to be treated and leads to another old adage about having something nice to say. Stop and think before you boast or criticise someone else. Give yourself a moment to think about how they would be affected in the same you would be when someone said the same thing to you. You have to hold firm to the idea of being open to other opinions and personalities. As long as you can find a way to relate to others and keep yourself from always putting on the arrogance or exploiting others, you can begin to see a change in yourself and how people around you now see you.

REPLACEMENT

Making new friends can be an important way to get a fresh start emotionally. You can knock out two birds with one stone and find an opportunity to get involved with the scene around you. For example, join a book club or start doing some hobby that you normally like. These can be majorly beneficial to your overall psyche and make you feel like you're worth something since you'll be constantly improving yourself, either getting better at a hobby or constantly picking up new knowledge and perspectives through literature. However, you'll also meet people with common interests and start to pick up some of the pieces and shrapnel that are left behind from the abusive relationship. While not everybody is going to be kind and receptive, it's almost certain that you're going to meet people who *are* genuine and kind and are a force worth having in your life.

This also swings back to yet another thing you need to do: work on your confidence. The truth is that, after an emotionally and verbally abusive relationship, you feel like you aren't worth anything, partly because you were even in that relationship at all. You start to wonder why anybody would treat you well if that person wouldn't even treat you well. The thing you need to understand, first and foremost, is that it isn't a problem with *you* or *your* worthiness. It ultimately comes down to a problem with the other person and their grand inability to cope with some trauma which happened to them long, long ago, or some skewed lineage of over-praise that led to them developing a superiority complex, or any other combination of things that could result in them being such a drastically bad and abusive person.

Understand that people are fragile, and nobody deserves to go through abuse. Despite that, your doubts about yourself are completely understandable. Know that they're unfounded. At the same time, start doing things that make you happy and make you feel as though you're improving yourself in order to improve your self-image in general.

STOP JUSTIFYING

The other step is to stop justifying your negative emotions. If you are getting angry all of the time, take responsibility for why and stop trying to place the blame elsewhere. Anger is a very powerful emotion, and it can quickly become a habit. As soon as you recognise that this habit is problematic and admit that it is not good, you can start to reevaluate why you are feeling this way so that you can change it.

STOP MAKING EXCUSES

When you make excuses for negative emotions, either for yourself or others, you are telling yourself that they are something out of your control. This is not true because you have the choice concerning how you react to a situation. If you continue to make excuses, you will never take responsibility for your behaviour. Over time, this can start to push people out of your life because they will not want to be around someone who cannot admit their faults or when they are wrong.

TAKE RESPONSIBILITY

Once you dedicate yourself to no longer making excuses, you can start to take some responsibility for how you act in various situations. This starts by taking the power away from your negative emotions. As you continue to take responsibility, you will find that they lose their hold over you. The right reactions and choices will naturally start to become easier to make.

STOP SAYING, "I CAN'T"

If you keep telling yourself that you cannot do something, you will eventually start to believe it. This is what's referred to as a self-fulfilling prophecy. Give yourself credit and stop limiting yourself to what is easy and in your comfort zone. As you push yourself and see how many things you are truly good at, this puts you in a more positive frame of mind, naturally pushing out the negative emotions.

I believe strongly in the power of self-healing, and I believe that any degree of emotional pain can be addressed through self-care and healing practices over time. It may be a long road and will certainly not be easy, but with proper support and belief in yourself, it is possible to move past the experience of narcissistic abuse to a large degree. You may not be able to erase the effects entirely, but it is possible to move and live a healthy, productive, and emotionally stable life after even the most damaging of emotional experiences. This is because the human brain has an incredible capacity to rewire itself and relearn how to live and love through healthy habits and new thought cycles that will take the place of the old, destructive thought cycles.

First of all, grab an old journal or buy yourself a nice new one.

Don't be afraid to lean on support sources. It is going to be very important, especially in the first few weeks or months following a traumatic emotional experience, to be able to lean on others for support. Perhaps, your experience with narcissist abuse has left you alienated from friends and/or family. Now is the time to reconnect with those loved ones. Don't be afraid. They are probably going to be so excited to have you back they won't even press you for details. Simply accept their support and love and lean on it when you need to. When you are ready, ask if you can discuss some of the details of your abuse as a way to process and move through them.

Educating yourself about narcissists and their tactics is going to be very important as you want to arm yourself against future abusers. If you feel you were too quick to trust in your last relationship, you may need to practice setting up barriers and waiting for people to prove to you that they are trustworthy. This may be difficult for those people who are naturally generous and giving of themselves emotionally. This can be a wonderful and amazing trait, but it is important to realise that not everyone you meet is going to have good intentions.

Finally, do what you can to cultivate a regular sleep schedule where you get at least 8 hours of sleep. Setting aside some time at night before bedtime for meditation may be a great way to help your brain settle down and prepare for rest. Try to go to bed at the same time every night and do something calming right before. Try not to eat and snack on junk food late at night as this will keep you up longer and may disrupt your sleep.

The nature of the self-healing journey is abstract and non-linear. It's not exactly a circle, rather more of a spiral. Healing and transformation take place in layers and octaves.

The journey gets so much better after the really heavy stuff is cleared. For the purposes of this book, I will put the stages in chronological order. As you apply these concepts to your life, notice how it flows similarly yet not always in exact linear order.

You might notice that you stayed stuck at a particular point and maybe even returned to earlier stages for a while before moving forward. Don't beat yourself up for this. These are tough lessons to resolve and integrate after the devastation of abuse. Keep in mind that this is a complex process. You could be surviving in one area of your life but still feeling victimised in another area or even thriving in some aspects.

MARKERS OF CHANGE

Document your progress so you can measure it and validate yourself. I highly recommend to journal during your recovery. It'll help you to weave pieces of your journey together. You will feel validated and a sense of accomplishment as you look back and notice how far you've come.

NEW BOUNDARIES

You'll be working to set and enforce new boundaries to protect yourself. Boundaries can be physical in terms of protecting your body and environment from certain people or situations. Boundaries can also be mental and emotional. These are trickier to see because they are invisible yet very important.

The most foundational boundary to start putting into place is the boundary of NO.

Start looking at where in your life you need to say NO. Where are you leaking energy from? Where are you giving too much and not receiving reciprocity in return? Where are you putting others' needs before your own? Start saying NO more often.

This may be the first time in your life that you give yourself permission to say NO. Perhaps since childhood you were conditioned to believe that you didn't have that right and if you did express your NO, you were likely punished. Now it's time to start re-wiring that programming by giving yourself permission to say NO when you need to.

Start noticing how others are affecting your thoughts and emotions. If you don't like how you feel after hanging out with someone or the thoughts that they planted in your mind with the words they said, start drawing new boundaries to not let that stuff in.

Chapter 14: Permit Self-Forgiveness

The power of forgiveness

One of the most important things you can do on your path to recovery to ensure your success is to forgive yourself and let go of those feelings of guilt and shame. It won't be easy to simply dismiss these feelings, especially if you've spent months or years listening to someone tell you you're not good enough or not smart or flawed in some way. This is going to take time to move away from, but it's important to make a daily habit of verbally or internally reaffirming that you are a survivor of narcissistic abuse and that you were strong enough to pull away.

Forgiveness is an act of power. It is also an effective way to release negative energy. If you carry hatred in your heart, then chances are that you will be filled with negativity. When you forgive, you not only do it for the person who is asking for forgiveness, but you also do it for your own good. In fact, forgiveness is possible even if the offender is not sorry for their wrongs against you. You can always forgive.

The following meditation technique is a good way to extend forgiveness to anyone. The steps are as follows:

- ☐ Sit or lie down comfortably. Close your eyes and visualise the person whom you want to forgive standing in front for you. Try to visualise the person as clearly as possible. Now raise your hands in the position of blessing with your hands facing outward. Think about the wrongs that the person has done to you but do not dwell on them. Just recall them into your mind. You do not even have to be attached to the memories. Now, find peace in your heart. Once you find this peace, state the name of the person whom you visualise and say, "(Name of the person), I forgive you."

- Forgiveness is an act of love. The more that you forgive, the more that you turn hatred into positive energy.

- As an empath, it may be easy for you to be offended. A common problem of being an empath is being overly sensitive. Negative energies may be able to affect you more than most people. If there is any person who seems to affect you negatively, you might want to extend forgiveness to them.

- Forgiveness is free. As such, you can extend forgiveness to everyone, even to those who do not feel sorry for offending you. The more that you forgive, the more that you free yourself from negative energy. If you do not forgive and allow the mistakes of others to fill you with hate, then you might end up just like them, or even worse.

- Forgiveness should be sincere. If you cannot find it in your heart to forgive a person, it helps if you spend some time to think about the situation. What is it that gives you a hard time to forgive someone? Sometimes by making reflections, we get to realise our own imperfections and faults.

☐ Once you realise the value of forgiveness, you will know just how effective it is in cleansing the soul. The more that you forgive, the more peaceful you will feel.

Another important part of forgiveness is learning how to forgive yourself. Indeed, there are people who carry lots of negative energy simply because they do not let go of it. Sometimes, to do this, you need to forgive yourself. You should learn to be kind to yourself. Unfortunately, in the modern world, it has become common to be hard on one's self. This is also why so many people are stressed out. Remember that you don't need to follow what society tells you. Be in control of your life. If something gives you more stress than you can manage, then you should do something about it. When you are an empath, you're more sensitive to stress. Of course, this doesn't mean that you should not face challenges. Rather, this means that you should be more in control, and you need to manage the level of stress that you are carrying.

Healing is important. Even if you are not an empath, you will find that you need to heal yourself from time to time. Healing is a natural part of life. No matter what you do, no matter how careful you try to be, it is inevitable that you will also face challenges and hardships along the way. It is also inevitable that you will have to deal with negative people from time to time. Hence, you will have to heal yourself when the need arises. Indeed, healing is a natural part of the life of an empath. A good thing about healing is that it transforms even negative energies into something that is much more positive. Indeed, healing and forgiveness can create a substantial positive impact on your life.

Taking care of your inner child

If you have subconscious childhood wounds, you probably developed defence mechanisms early on to cope with and adapt to grown up expectations. The behaviours or tendencies that you exhibit as an adult directly reflect this moulding.

Where you a relatively happy kid? But have you become a gloomy adult who's lonely or angry? Burdened by a bruised sense of self-worth?

When our parents aren't available to provide us with the proper nurturing, as children we experience anxiety and loss. We later develop accommodations to fill these wounds, which then morph into defence mechanisms for getting on with life, habits in our adulthood. This is what is commonly referred to as the FALSE SELF. Very many false-self personalities make an arsenal. From the funny ones, such as the class clown, to the angry ones, such as the bully, these personas have the ability to convince us we are what we in truth are NOT.

As we grow up and develop, we forget that this false-self character, the role we play for others (and sometimes even when alone with just yourself) is not who we really are, but the mind makes such a habit of being the false self that we take it to be all we are, nothing more, nothing else. We become so engrossed by the fantasy that we need our mask to continue being safe, even when it is no longer necessary, and even when it's done so much damage to others and to ourselves.

Some theorists say that we are always looking to reestablish our nurturing state, to find our symbiotic mothers in order to feel safe; much like when we were in the womb and had all our needs met automatically, without struggle, worry or anxiety. Of course, life isn't about regression and never will be, and that's where false-selves come into play. Assumed identities enable us to cope in public while we secretly burn with our failure to find a state of natural happiness once again. Most of the time, we find ourselves trying to trick others into filling these gaps. We look for mates who we tell ourselves will meet these needs. And when this fails, when these mates are unable or unwilling to meet our every need, to make us feel loved and safe at all times, it becomes the very root of relationship problems.

EXERCISE

Start doing body weight resistance exercises at home as well as cardio. If you live in an apartment, there are still things that you can do that shouldn't bother the people downstairs too much. For example, you can start running in order to get your cardio in and build up your strength and tonality. You can also start playing sports like basketball—though they may have never appealed to you before, sports can be a great and somewhat enjoyable way to pick up a hobby and start getting some exercise at the same time. They're also strangely therapeutic and will allow you to shut off your thoughts for a while and just get some positive endorphins flowing. If you can afford it, picking up a gym membership and then going three or four times a week can be a great way to start getting back into shape and improving your self-image.

There's a possibility that you aren't religious. If you aren't, then you can eschew this next bit of advice. However, if you are, you may find that diving into your spirituality and being active in a church community (or a community of whatever religion you're a part of) can lead to you developing vital friendships and getting to know people that you otherwise may not get to know. Also, spirituality can be a source of great solace for many people. It can be especially helpful to a lot of people to believe in something greater than themselves and you, if you're religious, are no exception. Even the act of praying - regardless of if the individual is secular or religious - has been scientifically proven to reduce stress levels and generally improve the disposition of the individual compared to how they were prior to praying at all.

If you have time in your schedule and can afford it, you may want to start going to a community college or going back to school if you don't have a degree. Getting a proper education and getting bigger paycheques, as a result, can lead to feeling like you're worth more than you are otherwise. On that same note, don't be afraid to find something to be passionate about. Don't just go home and watch TV and stagnate. You need something to push yourself forward. Find something you care about and start researching it. Start gardening or learning about something you've always been interested in. If you can do that, then you'll make a ton of extremely important progress.

In the end, the best things that you can do in order to heal are to better yourself and focus on yourself. Don't be afraid to spend a little extra to get a therapist or a gym membership, or even to treat yourself to a nice dinner once or twice per month. These things can be massively important parts of the healing process and can do a whole lot for helping you to feel better in general. You can do this— things will be better someday! Keep a smile on your face and fake it until you make it.

Chapter 15: The Narcissist healing cell

Healing is important. Even if you are not a narcissist, you will find that you need to heal yourself from time to time. Healing is a natural part of life. No matter what you do, no matter how careful you try to be, it is inevitable that you will also face challenges and hardships along the way. It is also inevitable that you will have to deal with negative people from time to time. Hence, you will have to heal yourself when the need arises. Indeed, healing is a natural part of the life of an empath. A good thing about healing is that it transforms even negative energies into something that is much more positive. Indeed, healing and forgiveness can create a substantial positive impact on your life.

During the first stage, denial is common. You do not want to believe that the narcissist in your life is a toxic person. You may make excuses for their behaviour and not want to admit that they are not healthy for you. Start writing down your thoughts concerning their treatment of you. Every few days, look back at what you wrote. This allows you to identify the pattern.

The second stage involves getting to know more about narcissism. This allows you to see what they do, and it allows you to realise that they are not capable of empathy and healthy relationships. This is a hard lesson to learn, but it is imperative for you to heal.

The third stage starts the separation process. Write a letter telling the narcissist in your life that you are walking away. Be detailed about why you are walking away. Now, you will not send the letter. This is for you to find some closure as you end the relationship.

For stage four, you cut the person from your life. Once you say "goodbye" you have to remain strong. Cut off all contact and do not give into them no matter what. It is common for a narcissist to try and manipulate you back into their life. You should consider a clean break. This means that you just cut off contact and never go back. Since this requires taking your attention away from them, expect them to try and contact you. They can be very persistent. Just make sure that you never respond.

Stage five involves taking a deep look at why you started a relationship with them in the first place. What was it about the narcissist that made you want them in your life? This can help you to prevent a future experience with a narcissist. It also lets you reflect and determine if your reasons for a relationship with them are things you need to work on. For example, was your self-esteem low when you started spending time with them? If so, improving your self-esteem can prevent a future narcissist experience.

The sixth stage is all about you. You want to evaluate your weaknesses and your self-worth. Find places that need improvement and dedicate yourself to working on them. After having a narcissist in your life, it is common to be in a negative place. Take small steps to essentially recover from your experience. Every person gets through their step in their own time. Do not rush and do not get discouraged if you are going through the motions slowly. Every day is another day without narcissism in your life.

The seventh and final stage is accepting that the situation happened and commit yourself to learning from it. Use the pain and negativity that the narcissist caused in your life to be stronger and to drive you to put the focus on self-care. You do not need anyone in your life that contributes anything negative. Remember this. You are valuable and worthy. You also want to truly forgive yourself.

The tendency toward narcissism is quite common, and it is present in all of us. At times, you might not know if someone has a particularly high degree of narcissism until you are deeply involved with them. Only then do you realise that all the traits you were attracted to are narcissistic qualities you cannot stand anymore. You might have a parent, a sibling, a partner, or even a friend who exhibits narcissistic traits, and you may be forced to deal or work along with them. It doesn't mean narcissists are unlovable; it merely makes it rather difficult to love them at times. People with high levels of narcissism might be fun, good at what they do, and quite charismatic and charming. If you have a say in the matter, you might like the idea of reforming narcissists instead of cutting off all ties with them. No two individuals are alike, and likewise, all narcissists aren't the same. So, the way you decide to handle a narcissist in your life will depend on the type of narcissist you are dealing with.

Conclusion

Thank you for making it through to the end of this book. Knowing more about what might feed a narcissistic personality gives you a greater insight into how to deal with your condition. You now have a better comprehension of what exactly defines a narcissist and the people they are. After determining the narcissists in you, dealing with the problem properly becomes imperative. It's important that you utilise the information here so that you can interact with people in the healthiest way possible. You now know that your personal self-esteem is important. Set yourself up with everything that you'll need to succeed in recovering your personality from NPD. Although you may not be able to completely cure NPD, it's possible to lead a full, rich life while dealing with the symptoms of NPD. The next step is to follow the tips in this book. Get a therapist. Start dealing with the maladaptive behaviours, either within yourself or your loved one. Most importantly, take care of yourself. You deserve to live a full, happy life, which can be a complicated thing when you or someone you love suffers from NPD. But you can start here. There is hope that life will get better.

Made in the USA
Coppell, TX
15 February 2022

73654339R00085